Cambridge Elements ≡

Elements in the Philosophy of Mathematics
edited by
Penelope Rush
University of Tasmania
Stewart Shapiro
The Ohio State University

ABSTRACTIONISM

Francesca Boccuni
Vita-Salute San Raffaele University

Luca Zanetti
Scuola Universitaria Superiore IUSS Pavia

CAMBRIDGE
UNIVERSITY PRESS

CAMBRIDGE
UNIVERSITY PRESS

Shaftesbury Road, Cambridge CB2 8EA, United Kingdom

One Liberty Plaza, 20th Floor, New York, NY 10006, USA

477 Williamstown Road, Port Melbourne, VIC 3207, Australia

314–321, 3rd Floor, Plot 3, Splendor Forum, Jasola District Centre,
New Delhi – 110025, India

103 Penang Road, #05–06/07, Visioncrest Commercial, Singapore 238467

Cambridge University Press is part of Cambridge University Press & Assessment,
a department of the University of Cambridge.

We share the University's mission to contribute to society through the pursuit of
education, learning and research at the highest international levels of excellence.

www.cambridge.org
Information on this title: www.cambridge.org/9781009509794

DOI: 10.1017/9781009375139

© Francesca Boccuni and Luca Zanetti 2024

First published 2024

A catalogue record for this publication is available from the British Library

ISBN 978-1-009-50979-4 Hardback
ISBN 978-1-009-37515-3 Paperback
ISSN 2399-2883 (online)
ISSN 2514-3808 (print)

Abstractionism

Elements in the Philosophy of Mathematics

DOI: 10.1017/9781009375139
First published online: December 2024

Francesca Boccuni
Vita-Salute San Raffaele University

Luca Zanetti
Scuola Universitaria Superiore IUSS Pavia

Author for correspondence: Luca Zanetti, luca.zanetti@iusspavia.it

Abstract: The aim of this Element is to provide an overview of abstractionism in the philosophy of mathematics. We shall distinguish between mathematical abstractionism, which interprets mathematical theories on the basis of abstraction principles, and philosophical abstractionism, which attributes a philosophical significance to mathematical abstractionism. We shall then survey the main semantic, ontological, and epistemological theses that are associated with philosophical abstractionism. We shall finally suggest that the most recent developments in the debate pull abstractionism in different directions.

Keywords: abstraction principles, foundations of mathematics, semantics of number expressions, mathematical knowledge, existence of mathematical objects

ISBNs: 9781009509794 (HB), 9781009375153 (PB), 9781009375139 (OC)
ISSNs: 2399-2883 (online), 2514-3808 (print)

Contents

1 Introduction

The aim of this Element is to provide an overview of *abstractionism* in the philosophy of mathematics.

As Cook (2021a) puts it,

> [a]bstraction is a process that begins via the identification of an equivalence relation on a class of entities – that is, a class of objects (or properties, or other sorts of "thing") is partitioned into equivalence classes based on some shared trait.[1]

Suppose, for instance, that some straight lines are drawn on a board, and they are then divided into collections (i.e. classes) based on whether they are parallel – parallelism is an equivalence relation. By doing so, we abstract away other features those lines might have, such as color. By this abstraction procedure, (abstract) objects corresponding to each equivalence class are finally introduced, which capture "what members of each equivalence class have in common" – in the example, directions.[2]

Along with Ebert and Rossberg (2016), we shall distinguish between *mathematical* and *philosophical* abstractionism. Mathematical abstractionism is the project of interpreting mathematical theories on the basis of *abstraction principles* (APs) and an underlying logic:

Definition 1 *An AP is the universal closure of a biconditional sentence with the following form:*

(AP) $\Sigma\alpha = \Sigma\beta \leftrightarrow \alpha \sim \beta$,

where α and β are variables of the same sort, Σ is a term-forming operator (which informally reads "the abstract of") that denotes a function from entities of the kind of α and β to entities of a (possibly) different kind, and $\sim$ is an equivalence relation over entities of the kind of α and β.

Philosophical abstractionism is any view that attributes a significance to mathematical abstractionism for the foundations of mathematics. The past few decades have witnessed a renewed interest in this particular foundational research. The resulting debate has engendered a varied landscape of views both on mathematical and philosophical abstractionism.

Mathematical and philosophical abstractionism are mutually entwined. The former may influence the perspective on the philosophy sustaining it.

---

[1] A relation R is an equivalence relation if, and only if, R is reflexive, symmetric, and transitive.
[2] Cook (2021a); see Mancosu (2016) for a historical overview.

Symmetrically, the philosophical significance attributed to APs may shape how mathematical abstractionism is carried out – and the (fragments of) mathematical theories that can be interpreted by abstraction.

Let's give an example. One of the most celebrated results of (contemporary) abstractionism is *Frege's Theorem*, which proves that the axioms of second-order Peano Arithmetic are derivable in second-order logic with *Hume's Principle* as the sole nonlogical axiom:

> The cardinal number of the Xs = the cardinal number of the Ys if, and only if, there is a bijection between X and Y.

As such, this theorem is a piece of mathematical abstraction: It shows that an alternative axiomatization of arithmetic is available, which conceives of natural numbers as finite cardinals rather than finite ordinals. At the same time, Frege's Theorem is central to the (Scottish) *Neologicist* view in the philosophy of mathematics, which attempts to provide a (semantic, epistemological, and ontological) foundation for arithmetical truths on the basis of Hume's Principle.[3] On the one hand, the success of Neologicism depends on Frege's Theorem and analogous results. These results show that Neologicism can aspire to be a philosophical account of (fragments of) *mathematics* as we know it. At the same time, much of the significance of Frege's Theorem comes from the philosophical views attached to it: Without these, second-order logic plus Hume's Principle is just an axiomatization of arithmetic on a philosophical par with others.

The relation between these two facets is reflected in the structure of this Element.

Section 2 will provide an overview of the main mathematical theories that APs can interpret. In particular, we will focus on Frege's original project, second-order Peano Arithmetic, real analysis, and set theory. The section will delve into further issues concerning the invariance of APs (Section 2.7) and the so-called *Bad Company problem* (Section 2.8).

Section 3 will present the main views on the semantics of abstract terms. We will focus particularly on the semantic role of numerical expressions, since the relevant literature concerns mainly them. Precisely, we will survey: the *substantival* view, ascribing singulartermhood to number words; the *adjectival* reading, which regards number words as modifiers of nouns; the *quantificational* perspective, conceiving of number words as numerical quantifiers. The section will provide also an overview of the *Caesar Problem* (Section 3.4).

---

[3] Scottish Neologicism is also labeled "neo-Fregeanism" (Hale and Wright 2001a) or simply "abstractionism" (Wright 2016, p. 161).

Section 4 will concern the predominant conceptions related to the ontology of abstraction. APs are often defended along with Platonism concerning abstracts. The latter usually relies on the existence of a realm of abstract objects mathematical theories describe, and on the idea that the existence and nature of such objects is independent of mathematicians. We will first show how abstractionists defend the existence claim, and then consider various ways in which the independence claim can be cashed out.

In Section 5, the most salient epistemological issues in the debate around APs will be discussed. In particular, we will focus on how epistemic access to abstract objects can be attained, and how APs themselves can be known, or at least blamelessly believed, as a result of their stipulation – which figures prominently in the Neologicist project.

Finally, Section 6 takes stock of the preceding discussion and looks at new waves in the abstractionist literature with a special emphasis on the relation between abstractionism and structuralism in the philosophy of mathematics.

2 Mathematical Abstractionism

2.1 Introduction

In the debate on abstractionism, APs can be conceived of as tools to achieve philosophical goals – whether foundational or not. Philosophical motivations notwithstanding, every abstractionist program relies on APs to interpret significant portions of mathematics. In this sense, the mathematical project comes first, and so we will treat it first. The reader mostly or exclusively concerned with the semantics, epistemology, and ontology of abstraction can skip to the relevant sections.

The most influential project originates with Frege. However, the axiomatic system in his *Grundgesetze der Arithmetik* (Frege 1893/1903) yields paradoxes. Later mathematical investigations into APs have aimed to strike a balance between consistency and mathematical strength. In particular, authors have focused on second-order Peano Arithmetic PA^2 (especially, Scottish Neologicists such as Crispin Wright and Bob Hale – Section 2.4); real analysis (e.g. Bob Hale and Stewart Shapiro – Section 2.5); set theory (particularly, George Boolos, Roy Cook, and Øystein Linnebo – Section 2.6).[4] All (or most) of such mathematical abstractionist theories are formulated in a language whose background logic is at least second-order – and usually classical. Hence, before presenting those theories, we provide an outline of second-order logic (Section 2.2), and of the inconsistency of Frege's *Grundgesetze* (Section 2.3).

---

[4] For a detailed survey, see e.g. Burgess (2005).

Sections 2.7 and 2.8 examine two major topics in abstractionism: the *invariance* of abstraction and the so-called *Bad Company problem*.

2.2 Second-Order Logic

The language $\mathscr{L}$ of second-order logic (SOL) contains, besides the language of first-order logic (FOL), an infinite list of n-adic second-order variables $X^n, Y^n, Z^n, \ldots$ varying over a second-order domain containing appropriate entities – that is, n-adic relations between first-order individuals; Fregean concepts and relations; or sets of (n-tuples of) first-order individuals – and existential and universal quantifiers binding second-order variables. The main logical principle of SOL is the *Comprehension Axiom* schema (CA):

$$\text{(CA)} \ \exists X^n \forall x_1, \ldots, x_n (X^n(x_1, \ldots, x_n) \leftrightarrow \phi(x_1, \ldots, x_n)),$$

where ϕ is any formula of $\mathscr{L}$ not containing X^n free. Every instance of CA, obtained by substituting ϕ by any formula of the language of SOL, is an axiom of SOL – that is, CA is an axiom *schema*.

CA states that there is a relation (or set) X^n such that all the individuals $x_1, \ldots, x_n$ are in the relation X^n (or are members of the n-tuples in the set X^n) if and only if $x_1, \ldots, x_n$ satisfy ϕ. Note that, if X is *monadic*, that is, it applies to just one individual at a time, X stands for a property, a Fregean concept, or a set of individuals. That ϕ is *any* formula of $\mathscr{L}$ implies that CA is *unrestricted*.

An *interpretation* of $\mathscr{L}$ consists in appropriate domains, and an assignment function. Let D_1 be a nonempty domain of individuals, which first-order variables vary over, and D_2 a nonempty domain containing n-adic relations between the individuals in D_1, which second-order variables vary over, for any positive integer n. In terms of sets, D_2 contains: sets of individuals of D_1; sets of pairs of individuals of D_1 (if X is dyadic); sets of triples of individuals of D_1 (if X is ternary); and so on. In case D_2 contains *all* such relations (sets), D_2 is the so-called *powerset* of D_1.[5] An interpretation of $\mathscr{L}$ that verifies every instance of CA is a *model* of $\mathscr{L}$.

In the *standard* semantics for $\mathscr{L}$, and therefore in the standard models of SOL, domain D_2 is the powerset of D_1. Once D_1 is fixed, D_2 will also be fixed without further specification. This is not necessarily so in *non*standard models of $\mathscr{L}$ – namely *Henkin models*. In Henkin models, D_2 may not contain all n-adic relations among individuals of D_1 (all subsets of D_1), since D_2 is just *a* nonempty set of subsets of D_1. Therefore, in Henkin models, it is necessary to fix both D_1 and D_2 explicitly.

---

[5] In other words, D_2 is the Cartesian product of D_1 with itself.

The model-theoretic properties of SOL may vary depending on whether the models considered are standard or not. A difference between standard and nonstandard models of SOL that is significant for the debate on abstraction (see Section 2.3 below) regards the cardinality of D_2, in case the first-order domain D_1 is infinite. Such a difference is more easily appreciated in terms of *Cantor's theorem*, proving that, for any set A, the cardinality of its powerset $\wp(A)$ is larger than the cardinality of A. In particular, if A has cardinality κ (formally, $|A| = \kappa$), then $|\wp(A)| = 2^\kappa$.[6] Since in the standard models of SOL D_2 is the powerset of D_1, if D_1 has cardinality κ, then D_2 has cardinality 2^κ by Cantor's theorem. Nonstandard models of SOL, on the other hand, are such that, if D_1 has infinite cardinality κ, D_2 may have cardinality that is less than 2^κ.[7]

2.3 Frege's *Grundgesetze der Arithmetik*

In *Grundgesetze der Arithmetik*, Frege relied on an AP embedded in a logical system that, for the sake of simplicity, can be assimilated to a higher-order logic,[8] with the aim of deriving substantial mathematical theories, such as arithmetic, real analysis and, possibly, complex analysis. The infamous AP Basic Law V (BLV) states that the extension of concept X is identical with the extension of concept Y if, and only if, every individual falling under X falls under Y and vice versa:

(BLV) $\quad \forall X \forall Y (\epsilon X = \epsilon Y \leftrightarrow \forall x (Xx \leftrightarrow Yx))$,[9]

where ϵ is the abstraction operator "the extension of."

---

[6] Let A be either a finite or infinite set. Assume that there is a bijection f between A and $\wp(A)$, such that each member of A is associated by f with exactly one member of $\wp(A)$, and vice versa. Let B contain the members of A not belonging to the subsets of A that f associates with them: (1) $y \in B \leftrightarrow y \notin f(y)$. Since B is a subset of A, by assumption there must be a member of A that f associates with B. Hence, for some member u of A: (2) $B = f(u)$. It follows (3) $y \in f(u) \leftrightarrow y \notin f(y)$. Since y and u are arbitrary members of A, y can be substituted by u, without loss of generality, so that (4) $u \in f(u) \leftrightarrow u \notin f(u)$: contradiction. Thus, there is no bijection f between A and $\wp(A)$. This implies that $|A| \neq |\wp(A)|$. Since it is impossible that $|A| > |\wp(A)|$, otherwise there would be a bijection between a subset of A and $\wp(A)$, it must be the case that $|A| < |\wp(A)|$. Precisely, since f is the characteristic function of A (i.e. f maps all elements of any subset B of A in the set $\{0, 1\}$: for every $x \in A$ and $B \subseteq A, f(x) = 1$ if $x \in B$; $f(x) = 0$, otherwise), if the cardinality of A is κ, the cardinality of $\wp(A)$ is 2^κ.

[7] For details on the syntax, semantics, and model-theoretic properties of SOL, see e.g. Shapiro (1991) and Väänänen (2021).

[8] See Cook (2023) for a survey on the peculiarities of Frege's logic.

[9] Generally, Frege speaks of *value-ranges* of functions – see e.g. Cook (2023) and Zalta (2023). For the sake of simplicity, we will use "extension," which corresponds to Frege's notion of "extension of a concept." Notably, the extension operator ϵ can be either functional (i.e. binding second-order variables, as BLV) or variable-binding (i.e. taking *formulæ* as arguments: $\epsilon x.\phi x = \epsilon x.\psi x \leftrightarrow \forall x (\phi x \leftrightarrow \psi x)$).

The axiomatic system consisting in unrestricted SOL and BLV is inconsistent. This is easily seen by proving so-called *Russell's paradox* – in a Fregean spirit, we will talk of concepts and extensions, but the same applies to properties and sets. First of all, the existence of the "Russellian" concept "being the extension of a concept under which that very extension does not fall" is guaranteed by the following instance of (unrestricted) CA:

$$\exists X \forall y (Xy \leftrightarrow \exists Y (y = \epsilon Y \wedge \neg Yy)). \tag{2.1}$$

Call such a concept "$\mathcal{R}$". Since it is a theorem of Frege (1893/1903) that for every concept there is the corresponding extension, the extension $\epsilon \mathcal{R}$ must exist.

Let us assume that $\epsilon \mathcal{R}$ falls under $\mathcal{R}$: $\mathcal{R}(\epsilon \mathcal{R})$. Then, $\epsilon \mathcal{R}$ satisfies the formula defining $\mathcal{R}$:

$$\exists Y (\epsilon \mathcal{R} = \epsilon Y \wedge \neg Y(\epsilon \mathcal{R})). \tag{2.2}$$

Equation (2.2) implies $\epsilon \mathcal{R} = \epsilon Z$, for Z instantiating Y. By instantiating the left-to-right direction of BLV with $\mathcal{R}$ and Z

$$\epsilon \mathcal{R} = \epsilon Z \rightarrow \forall x (\mathcal{R}x \leftrightarrow Zx), \tag{2.3}$$

it must hold that $\forall x (\mathcal{R}x \leftrightarrow Zx)$, stating that every object x falls under $\mathcal{R}$ if, and only if, it falls under Z. The latter, along with $\neg Z(\epsilon \mathcal{R})$, implies that $\epsilon \mathcal{R}$ does not fall under $\mathcal{R}$, namely $\neg \mathcal{R}(\epsilon \mathcal{R})$. Therefore,

$$\mathcal{R}(\epsilon \mathcal{R}) \rightarrow \neg \mathcal{R}(\epsilon \mathcal{R}). \tag{2.4}$$

Let us now assume that $\epsilon \mathcal{R}$ does not fall under $\mathcal{R}$: $\neg \mathcal{R}(\epsilon \mathcal{R})$. By the definition of $\mathcal{R}$, the latter implies

$$\neg \exists Y (\epsilon \mathcal{R} = \epsilon Y \wedge \neg Y(\epsilon \mathcal{R})). \tag{2.5}$$

By the usual transformations of logical connectives and quantifiers, it follows that

$$\forall Y (\epsilon \mathcal{R} = \epsilon Y \rightarrow Y(\epsilon \mathcal{R})). \tag{2.6}$$

Equation (2.6) implies $\epsilon \mathcal{R} = \epsilon \mathcal{R} \rightarrow \mathcal{R}(\epsilon \mathcal{R})$ by universal instantiation. Since by identity $\epsilon \mathcal{R} = \epsilon \mathcal{R}$, it must hold that $\mathcal{R}(\epsilon \mathcal{R})$. So,

$$\neg \mathcal{R}(\epsilon \mathcal{R}) \rightarrow \mathcal{R}(\epsilon \mathcal{R}). \tag{2.7}$$

Finally, since if $\mathcal{R}(\epsilon \mathcal{R})$, then $\neg \mathcal{R}(\epsilon \mathcal{R})$, and if $\neg \mathcal{R}(\epsilon \mathcal{R})$, then $\mathcal{R}(\epsilon \mathcal{R})$, it must be the case that

$$\mathcal{R}(\epsilon \mathcal{R}) \leftrightarrow \neg \mathcal{R}(\epsilon \mathcal{R}) : contradiction. \tag{2.8}$$

Both unrestricted CA and BLV are involved in the derivation of Russell's paradox in Frege (1893/1903).[10] A famous debate between Boolos (1993) and Dummett (1994) concerns its origin.

On the one hand, Boolos blamed it on BLV and its inconsistent requirement that for every concept, there is exactly one extension corresponding to it, which violates Cantor's theorem.[11]

On the other hand, Dummett (1991, 1994) blames the contradiction on the *impredicativity* of CA: Since CA is unrestricted, second-order variables may appear on its right-hand side in the scope of a second-order quantifier, that is, they are *bound*. The logic underlying Frege (1893/1903) is classical, so it requires that the (first- or second-order) domain be a "definite totality," given once and for all. Still, by quantifying over the second-order domain, more and more Fregean concepts (properties or sets) can be defined. Hence, the second-order domain grows larger and larger, deeming it no definite totality after all.

Consider for instance the concept "being an extension," formally introduced by the instance of CA $\exists X \forall x(Xx \leftrightarrow \exists Y(x = \epsilon Y))$ – in a language containing the abstraction operator ϵ – and call it "$\mathcal{E}$". Concept $\mathcal{E}$ must have an extension ($\epsilon\mathcal{E}$), but then also $\epsilon\mathcal{E}$ must fall under $\mathcal{E}$. But if concepts are "identical" just in case exactly the same objects fall under them, then the concept "being an extension" we started from is different from the concept "being an extension" we ended up with. This process never ends, that is, as Dummett argues, there are *indefinitely extensible* concepts, which are such that "if we can form a definite conception of a totality all of whose members fall under that concept, we can, by reference to that totality, characterize a larger totality all of whose members fall under it."[12]

To some extent, both Boolos and Dummett are right: there are consistent axiomatic systems of unrestricted SOL with restricted BLV;[13] but also unrestricted BLV plus restricted (classical) SOL may have models. So, in general, a philosophically meaningful question concerns what the best way out of the paradox is. Broadly speaking, two solutions can be envisaged, each of which modify

---

[10] For a detailed proof of the inconsistency in Frege (1893/1903), see e.g. Zalta (2023).

[11] In Fine's (2002) words, BLV is "inflationary": The abstraction function ϵ requires that D_2 be injected into D_1; therefore, it requires that the partition of D_2 induced by the equivalence relation $\leftrightarrow$ on the right-hand side of BLV has the same cardinality as D_1 *contra* Cantor's theorem. See also e.g. Uzquiano (2019). Still, see Paseau (2015) for the view that the inconsistency in Frege (1893/1903) does not rely on cardinality issues.

[12] Dummett (1993, p. 441).

[13] Not to mention that pure (classical) unrestricted SOL has models.

either SOL or BLV, one way or another.[14] However, such solutions to the inconsistency may affect the mathematical strength of the resulting theory. In what follows, we will focus on the fragments of mathematics that can be interpreted by consistent APs, but connections to the solutions to the inconsistency of Frege's system will emerge.

2.4 Arithmetical Abstraction

Scottish Neologicism (Hale and Wright 2001a, Wright 1983) is a radical and very influential solution to the inconsistency of Frege (1893/1903) substituting BLV by a consistent AP strong enough to interpret second-order Peano Arithmetic PA^2,[15] namely *Hume's Principle*

(HP) $\forall X \forall Y (\#X = \#Y \leftrightarrow X \approx Y)$,

while keeping SOL unrestricted. HP reads informally, "The number of the Xs is identical with the number of the Ys if, and only if, X and Y are equinumerous" – where $\#$ is the cardinality operator "the number of." Precisely, the formula "$X \approx Y$" abbreviates the (purely second-order) statement that there is a relation R such that every object falling under X is R-related to a unique object falling under Y, and for every object falling under Y there's a unique object falling under X that is R-related to it:

($\approx$) $X \approx Y \leftrightarrow_{def} \exists R \, (\forall x \, (X(x) \rightarrow \exists! y \, (Y(y) \land R(x,y))) \land \forall x \, (Y(x) \rightarrow \exists! y \, (X(y) \land R(y,x))))$,

with "$\exists! x \, \phi(x)$" defined as: $\exists x (\phi(x) \land \forall y \, (\phi(y) \rightarrow x = y))$.

In unrestricted SOL with HP as its sole nonlogical axiom, a formulation of Frege's definitions of the arithmetical notions necessary to derive PA^2 can be provided without the need for BLV. The resulting axiomatic system is *Frege Arithmetic* (FA). Frege Arithmetic has a model in the natural numbers (Boolos 1987a) and interprets PA^2 (Boolos and Heck 1998). The latter result is now known as *Frege's Theorem*.

---

[14] Once he was made aware of the inconsistency, Frege mended his axiomatization by restricting BLV. However, his attempt, now known as *Frege's way out*, is still hopelessly problematic. See Cook (2019) and Quine (1955).

[15] PA^2 is the axiomatic theory whose language is that of SOL augmented by an individual constant "0" and a unary function s. Its axioms are

(A1) $\forall x (0 \neq sx)$, stating that 0 is no successor;

(A2) $\forall xy (sx = sy \rightarrow x = y)$, stating that the successor function s is injective;

(A3) $\forall x \exists y (sx = y)$, stating that every natural number has a successor;

(A4) $\forall X (X0 \land \forall x (Xx \rightarrow X(sx))) \rightarrow \forall x Xx)$, i.e. the mathematical induction axiom stating that for all X, in case 0 is X, and for all natural numbers x, the successor of x is X if x is X, then all natural numbers are X.

The language of FA consists in the language of SOL augmented by the primitive term-forming operator #, which applies to second-order variables (or constants) – the resulting expressions are singular terms. Of course, every (appropriate) complex formula of such a language corresponds to a concept, since CA is unrestricted. By adopting the notational convention that a concept defined by a formula ϕ is denoted by "$[x.\phi(x)]$" Frege's definitions can be formulated in the language of SOL plus HP:

(Zero) $0 =_{def} \#[x.x \neq x]$,

which defines 0 as the number of the concept *not self-identical*;

(Predecessor) $P(x,y) \leftrightarrow_{def} \exists X \exists u(Xu \wedge y = \#X \wedge x = \#[z.Xz \wedge z \neq u])$,

stating that x *precedes* y just in case there's a nonempty concept X such that y is its number and x is the number of the concept *falling under X but for one individual*;

(Hereditary) $Her(X,R) \leftrightarrow_{def} \forall x,y(R(x,y) \wedge Xx \rightarrow Xy))$,

defining the notion of *X being hereditary in the relation R* just in case, if R holds between x,y, and x is X, then y is X;

(Ancestral) $R^*(x,y) \leftrightarrow_{def} \forall X(\forall z(R(x,z) \rightarrow Xz) \wedge Her(X,R) \rightarrow Xy)$,

that is, Frege's famous definition of the *ancestral of a relation* (Frege 1879), which states that y is X, if (i) for all z, is X if R holds of x,z, and (ii) X is hereditary in R.

(Weak Ancestral) $R^+(x,y) \leftrightarrow_{def} R^*(x,y) \vee x = y$,

according to which x,y stand in the weak ancestral of relation R just in case either the ancestral of R holds of x,y or x,y are identical;

(Natural Number) $\mathbb{N}x \leftrightarrow_{def} P^+(0,x)$,

stating that x is a natural number just in case x belongs to the series of individuals starting with 0 and determined by the weak ancestral of the predecessor.[16]

By the underlying SOL, HP, and previous definitions, (appropriate formulations of) second-order Peano axioms are derivable.

---

[16] A different approach to HP than Scottish Neologicism is in Tennant's (*Constructive* or) *Natural Logicism*, i.e. a constructively acceptable theory of abstraction based on Gentzen-style introduction and elimination rules for abstraction operators. In particular, Tennant (1987, 2022) rephrase HP as:

(Schema N) $\#x.\phi x = \bar{n} \leftrightarrow \exists_n x \phi x$,

Is there any consistent formulation of (SOL plus) BLV that, analogously to HP, interprets arithmetic? The answer may depend upon how large a fragment of arithmetic is at stake. A first group of theories (Table 1; for an explanation of the axioms in Table 1, see Table 2) interprets at most *Robinson Arithmetic* $\mathcal{Q}$, which is weaker than first-order Peano Arithmetic PA:[17]

Table 1 Consistent subsystems of SOL plus BLV: Robinson Arithmetic

Background logic	Formulation of BLV	
FOL	(BLV$_S$) $\epsilon x.\phi x = \epsilon x.\psi x$ $\leftrightarrow \forall x(\phi x \leftrightarrow \psi x)$	Schroeder-Heister (1987); Parsons (1987); Burgess (1998)
(CA$_P$) $\exists X \forall y(Xy \leftrightarrow \phi y)$	BLV or BLV$_S$	Heck (1996)
(Δ_1^1-CA) $\forall x(\phi x \leftrightarrow \psi x)$ $\rightarrow \exists Y \forall x(Yx \leftrightarrow \phi x)$	BLV or BLV$_S$	Wehmeier (1999); Ferreira and Wehmeier (2002)

where the left-to-right direction is the elimination rule for $\#$, and the right-to-left direction is the introduction rule for $\#$. Tennant's proposal relies on a free relevant intuitionistic logic – for overviews on free, relevant, and intuitionistic logics, see Nolt (2021), Antonelli (2010a), and Iemhoff (2020), respectively. Also, Shapiro and Linnebo (2015) make use of intuitionistic FOL with identity plus HP in order to derive *Heyting Arithmetic*, i.e. the intuitionistic version of Peano axioms. Heck (2011b) proposes a possible axiomatization of HP, called *Arché Arithmetic*, that relies, strictly speaking, on (classical) first-order syntactic resources and intro-duction/elimination rules, but has enough mathematical strength to derive Frege's Theorem. Schindler (2021) utilizes a formulation of Schema N, called *Numerical Equivalence Schema* (NES), for supporting a *minimalist* account of numbers according to which NES suffices to explain all facts about them – see Section 4.2.

[17] See e.g. Burgess (2005, chapter 2), Walsh (2016), and Visser (2009), and Ganea (2007). The language of Robinson's $\mathcal{Q}$ is the language of FOL with identity augmented by an individual constant "0," a unary function s, and the binary functions $+, \times$. Along with axioms A1, A2, and A3 of PA^2 (see footnote 15), the axioms of $\mathcal{Q}$ are the recursive axioms for addition and multiplication:

(Q1) $\forall x(x + 0 = x)$;
(Q2) $\forall xy(x + sy = s(x + y))$;
(Q3) $\forall x(x \times 0 = 0)$;
(Q4) $\forall xy(x \times sy = (x \times y) + x)$.

The language of PA is the same as the language of Robison's $\mathcal{Q}$, and its axioms are the same as $\mathcal{Q}$'s plus the axiom schema of mathematical induction:

(Ind) $\phi 0 \wedge \forall x(\phi x \rightarrow \phi(sx)) \rightarrow \forall x \phi x$,

where ϕ is a metavariable varying over the formulæ of the language of PA.

Table 2 Axioms in Table 1

BLV$_S$	Since FOL lacks second-order quantification, BLV must be *schematic* – hence the subscript S – with metavariables ϕ, ψ for formulæ of the underlying language.
CA$_P$	ϕ contains neither X free nor bound second-order variables at all. If so restricted, CA is *predicative* – hence the subscript P.
Δ_1^1-CA	A formula is Σ_1^1 (Π_1^1) if it has the form $\exists X\phi$ ($\forall X\phi$) and ϕ contains no second-order quantifier. Δ_1^1-CA requires that, in order to appear on its right-hand side, a formula ϕ must be at most a Σ_1^1-formula provably equivalent to a Π_1^1-formula ψ.

In general, if CA is restricted to Σ_1^1- or Π_1^1-formulæ, CA plus BLV in either form is inconsistent. It is not known whether there are intermediate consistent Δ_1^1-CA and Σ_1^1/Π_1^1-CA.

Though not at all trivial, Robinson's $\mathscr{Q}$ is still a rather small fragment of arithmetic, especially compared to Frege's original goal. In order to interpret larger parts of arithmetic by BLV, the theories in Table 1 have to be revised.

In Antonelli and May (2005), an axiom system containing unrestricted CA and restricted BLV that interprets PA is presented, where numbers are conceived of as *concepts* of objects. In order to define cardinals as equivalence classes of equinumerous concepts, extensions (value-ranges) are needed: (concept) N is a number if, and only if, there is a concept X such that an object x falls under N if, and only if, x is the value-range of a concept equinumerous to X. Such an object is called a *witness* of N. A conditional formulation of BLV is provided:

$$\forall X\forall Y\forall x\forall y(VR(X,x) \wedge VR(Y,y) \rightarrow (\forall z(Xz \leftrightarrow Yz) \leftrightarrow x = y)), \qquad (2.9)$$

where $VR(X,x)$ means "x is the value-range of X." (2.9) does not guarantee that value-ranges exist. To correct this, Antonelli and May's (2005) system contains also a further axiom:

$$\forall x(\phi x \rightarrow \exists X(Nn(X) \wedge Wtn(X,x))) \rightarrow \exists x VR(\phi,x), \qquad (2.10)$$

where Nn is the predicate "being a natural number," and Wtn is the relation of x being a witness of X. This axiom guarantees that, for any formula ϕ applying exclusively to witnesses of natural numbers, there is a value-range.[18]

---

[18] For a similar approach to, and also relevant differences with, Antonelli and May (2005), see Demopoulos and Bell (1993).

Consistent systems as the ones in Ferreira (2018), Boccuni (2010, 2013) in Table 3 (for an explanation of the axioms in Table 3, see Table 4) interpret PA^2 by adding a further round of higher-order variables (and comprehension axioms thereof) to SOL, and calibrating the restrictions on BLV or BLV$_S$. The language of the axiomatic theory in Ferreira (2018) consists in: impredicative second-order variables $\mathscr{X}, \mathscr{Y}, \mathscr{Z}, \ldots$ varying over impredicative concepts; predicative second-order variables $X, Y, Z, \ldots$ varying over predicatively definable concepts; and the variable-binding operator ϵ. The language of the axiomatic theory in Boccuni (2010, 2013) adds to regular second-order quantification quantifiers binding *plural variables* $xx, yy, zz, \ldots$ governed by (unrestricted) *plural logic*,[19] and the functional operator ϵ.

Table 3 Consistent subsystems of SOL plus BLV: PA^2

Background logic	Formulation of BLV	
$(CA_{Imp})\ \exists\mathscr{X}\forall y(\mathscr{X}y \leftrightarrow \phi y)$	$(BLV_S)\ \epsilon x.\phi x = \epsilon x.\psi x$	Ferreira (2018)
$(CA_P)\ \exists X\forall y(Xy \leftrightarrow \psi y)$	$\leftrightarrow \forall x(\phi x \leftrightarrow \psi x)$	
$(CA_{PL})\ \exists xx\forall y(y \prec xx \leftrightarrow \phi y)$	$(BLV)\ \forall X\forall Y(\epsilon X = \epsilon Y$	Boccuni (2010, 2013)
$(CA_P)\ \exists X\forall y(Xy \leftrightarrow \psi y)$	$\leftrightarrow \forall x(Xx \leftrightarrow Yx))$	

Table 4 Axioms in Table 3

CA_{Imp}	ϕ is unrestricted.
CA_P	ψ does not contain either X free or bound predicative second-order variables or impredicative second-order variables at all.
BLV_S	No formula in the scope of ϵ contains impredicative second-order variables at all.
CA_{PL}	ϕ is unrestricted.
CA_P	X varies over Fregean concepts, and ψ contains neither bound second-order variables nor free plural variables.
BLV	X, Y are concepts definable by CA_P.

---

[19] Plural logic was initially proposed by Boolos (1984, 1985) as an ontologically innocent interpretation of SOL, which, later on, has been developed in dedicated formal systems and semantics – see e.g. Florio and Linnebo (2021) and Linnebo (2022) for extensive surveys. In Boolos's semantics, second-order variables are interpreted as ranging over individuals considered *plurally*, rather than over sets or properties. Boolos (1985) provides truth-clauses for second-order formulæ on the basis of an interpretation consisting in a pair $< R, D_1 >$, where R is an assignment relation mapping second-order variables to zero or more individuals of the first-order domain D_1. No domain D_2 is postulated.

Ferreira's (2018) system not only interprets PA^2, but it does so by FA. Boccuni (2010, 2013) interprets PA^2, but because of the restrictions imposed on BLV, it falls short of providing the definitions needed to recover FA.[20]

2.5 Real Number Abstraction

A further mathematical theory abstractionists have been interested in interpreting via abstraction is real analysis.[21] Frege himself devoted Part III of the second volume of *Grundgesetze* to a theory of ratios of magnitudes, which was Frege's way of conceiving of real numbers and which he left unfinished in the wake of Russell's paradox.[22]

More recently, further attempts to recover real analysis by abstraction are investigated in, for example, Shapiro (2000), Hale (2000), Roeper (2020), and Boccuni and Panza (2022). We will consider Hale's and Shapiro's proposals.

Shapiro (2000) provides a piecemeal reconstruction of abstractionist real analysis, starting from natural numbers as introduced by HP, and proceeding by several APs. First, *integers* as abstract objects are defined over differences between pairs of natural numbers a, b, c, d:

---

[20] For a similar strategy targeting HP, see e.g. Roeper (2016), where "$\#X$" stands for a (reified) numerical property of the plurality X. In Boccuni (2010, 2013), not every plurality corresponds to an extension. For a similar strategy (with nominalized predicates), see Cocchiarella (1985, 1992).

[21] The language of real analysis is the language of FOL with identity augmented by the individual constants "0" and "1," the binary functions $+, \times$, the unary functions $-, ^{-1}$, and the binary predicate $\leq$. The function $-$ yields a negative real number; the function $^{-1}$ yields the inverse of a real number, e.g. x^{-1} is $\frac{1}{x}$. We provide nonformal formulations of the axioms of real analysis:

(A1) Addition and multiplication are associative and commutative.
(A2) Multiplication distributes over addition.
(A3) 0 is not equal to 1.
(A4) Additive identity: Every real number added to 0 equals itself.
(A5) Multiplicative identity: Every real number multiplied by 1 equals itself.
(A6) Existence of additive inverses: For every real number x, there's a real number $-x$ such that adding x to $-x$ equals 0.
(A7) Existence of multiplicative inverses: For every real number x other than 0, there is a real number x^{-1} such that multiplying x by x^{-1} equals 1.
(A8) $\leq$ is a total order over the set of real numbers $\mathbb{R}$.
(A9) The order $\leq$ is preserved under addition and multiplication.
(A10) Dedekind-Completeness: If A is a nonempty subset of $\mathbb{R}$, and if A has an upper bound in $\mathbb{R}$, then A has a least upper bound u such that, for every upper bound v of A, $u \leq v$,

where x is an upper bound of A if, and only if, for every y in A, x is greater than or equal to y; and x is the least upper bound of A in $\mathbb{R}$ if, and only if, x is the greatest real number that is less than or equal to any number in A.

[22] For exhaustive introductions and commentary, besides Frege (1893/1903, Vol. II, Part III), see also e.g. Dummett (1991, chapter 22), Simons (1987), Schirn (2013, 2023), and Snyder and Shapiro (2019).

(DIF) $INT < a, b >= INT < c, d > \leftrightarrow (a + d) = (b + c).$[23]

Addition and multiplication for integers can be defined by the underlying unrestricted SOL.

Secondly, *quotients* of pairs of integers m, n, p, q are introduced by the AP

(QUOT) $Q < m, n >= Q < p, q > \leftrightarrow ((n = 0 \land q = 0) \lor (n \neq 0 \land q \neq 0 \land m \times q = n \times p)).$

Rational numbers are quotients $Q < m, n >$ for $n \neq 0.$[24]

Finally, by defining addition and multiplication for rationals, and the relation "less than" ($\leq$), an AP for *cuts* is introduced:

(CUT) $\forall P \forall Q (C(P) = C(Q) \leftrightarrow \forall r (P \leq r \leftrightarrow Q \leq r)),$

where $P \leq r$ holds between a concept P of rationals and a rational r if, and only if, r is an upper bound of P. Say that P is *bounded*, if $P \leq r$ holds. A *real number* is a cut $C(P)$, for P bounded and nonempty. Shapiro's (2000) reconstruction delivers nondenumerably many cuts forming a totally ordered and Dedekind-complete field – that is, real analysis is recovered. Still, such a construction has a "decidedly *structural* feel" – Ebert and Rossberg (2016, p. 14, italics in the original).

Hale (2000, 2002, 2005) provides a reconstruction of real analysis, which is more Fregean in spirit, since Hale's proposal is to define real numbers as abstract objects defined over pairs of magnitudes.[25] The AP

(RATIO) $\mathscr{R}a\ell < a, b >= \mathscr{R}a\ell < c, d > \leftrightarrow \forall m \forall n (ma \lesseqqgtr nb \leftrightarrow mc \lesseqqgtr nd),$

where $\mathscr{R}a\ell$ is an abstraction operator mapping ordered pairs of magnitudes a, b, c, d to objects (ratios of quantities, i.e. reals), and m, n are positive integers, states that the ratio of a to b is the same as that of c to d if, and only if, any positive integer multiple of a is equal to, greater than, or less than any positive integer multiple of b if, and only if, the same holds of the corresponding multiples of c and d.

---

[23] $< a, b >, < c, d >$ are governed by a principle PAIR, stating that the ordered pair $< a, b >$ is identical with the ordered pair $< c, d >$ if, and only if, a is identical with c and b is identical with d.

[24] Since m, n, p, q are *any* integers, they might also be 0. The first disjunct $n = 0 \land q = 0$ covers the instances of the form $Q(m, 0) = Q(p, 0)$ – for any integers m, p. In particular, what the first disjunct does is just to guarantee that all those quotients are identical to each other and nothing else – whatever they might be. This, along with the second disjunct, implies that the right-hand side of QUOT is an equivalence relation. We thank Stewart Shapiro for clarifying this to us.

[25] See also e.g. Wright (2000). See Batitsky (2002) and Panza and Sereni (2019) for discussion.

A few issues arise from Hale's reconstruction: For example, does the resulting theory imply the existence of nondenumerably many magnitudes, in order to deliver the existence of nondenumerably many reals?[26] Is the equivalence relation on the right-hand side of RATIO definable in purely logical terms?

We mentioned Shapiro's abstractionist reconstruction of reals is taken to have a "structural feel," as opposed to Hale's, which is more Fregean in spirit. In order to adjudicate between such different conceptions of real numbers, the so-called *Frege's (applicability) Constraint* (FC) has been invoked. According to FC:

> a satisfactory foundation for a mathematical theory must somehow build its applications, actual and potential, into its core – into the content it ascribes to the statements of the theory – rather than merely "patch them on from the outside".[27]

A structural conception of the reals such as Shapiro's is based on Dedekind's cuts,[28] as opposed to an abstractionist construction according to which reals are ratios of magnitudes. But, if the main applications of real numbers are for measuring quantities, such as, for example, masses, temperatures, or lengths, reals as Dedekind's cuts fail FC, whereas abstractionist definitions such as the one provided by RATIO satisfy applicability, since RATIO has the applications to magnitudes built in its right-hand side.[29,30]

2.6 Set Abstraction

So far, we have seen how much arithmetic and real analysis can be recovered via different APs and some formulation of SOL. It is time we address a further worry, which was not in Frege's purview, but is indeed a concern for many

---

[26] See e.g. Hale (2005) for this issue and further conditions magnitudes must satisfy for RATIO to yield reals.

[27] Wright (2000, p. 324).

[28] See e.g. Reck (2020).

[29] See Wright (2000) and Hale (2002, 2005). According to Neologicists, FC applies not just to real analysis but also in general, e.g. arithmetic. A structuralist conception of natural numbers as finite ordinals (in general, an ordinal number is a set totally ordered by the set-theoretic membership relation ∈ and such that all its members are also its subsets), as opposed to an abstractionist view according to which natural numbers are finite cardinals, unlike the latter fails FC. For discussion, see Panza and Sereni (2019), Sereni (2019) and Heck (2000, 1997a). For a structuralist reply, see Snyder, Samuels, and Shapiro (2018).

[30] There are no explicit attempts in current abstractionism to define complex numbers by abstraction, though remarks on complex analysis can be found in the literature on structural APs as in e.g. Litland (2022) and Wigglesworth (2018) – see also footnote 40. Though Frege did not get to a formalization of complex analysis in Frege (1893/1903), there is evidence that he had in mind its formal investigation – see e.g. Tappenden (2019, 1995), Schirn (2023), and Brandom (1996).

current abstractionist programs: How much of contemporary set theory, that is, Zermelo-Fraenkel set theory augmented with the axiom of choice (ZFC), can be interpreted by abstraction?

ZFC is an axiomatic set theory usually expressed in FOL with identity, augmented by the primitive nonlogical constant $\in$ (for *set membership*), and whose intended interpretation is a nonempty collection of sets.

ZFC is taken to capture the *iterative conception of sets*: roughly, by axiomatically postulating the existence of some basic sets, more and more sets are formed through stages by the iterated application of operations among sets available in the set-theoretic universe. This procedure gives rise to a *cumulative hierarchy* of sets that is *open-ended*: there is no final stage of set formation. It is now customary to call such a hierarchy "V."[31]

The axioms of ZFC are:

(Extensionality) $\forall x \forall y (x = y \leftrightarrow \forall z (z \in x \leftrightarrow z \in y))$,

stating that any sets x, y are identical just in case they contain exactly the same members;

(Separation) $\forall z \exists x \forall y (y \in x \leftrightarrow y \in z \wedge \phi y)$,

where ϕ does not contain x free, stating that, for any given set z, there is a set x containing all individuals y that are members of z and satisfy the formula ϕ;

(Empty Set) $\exists x \forall y (y \in x \leftrightarrow y \neq y)$,

stating the existence of the empty set. Since Extensionality guarantees that there is a unique empty set, the individual constant "$\emptyset$" can be explicitly defined in the language of ZFC;

(Pairing) $\forall x \forall y \exists z \forall u (u \in z \leftrightarrow u = x \vee u = y)$,

stating that there is a set containing two elements;[32]

(Foundation) $\forall x (\exists y (y \in x) \rightarrow \exists y (y \in x \wedge \neg \exists z (z \in y \wedge z \in x)))$,

---

[31] Formally, the stages of the set-theoretic universe are described as follows: There is an initial stage V_0, which can be empty or contain *ur*-elements, i.e. individuals that are not sets; the successor stage $V_{\alpha+1}$ is the powerset of V_α; the limit stage, roughly a stage that is no successor to any stage, is the union of all the previous stages (i.e. $V_\lambda = \bigcup_{\alpha < \lambda} V_\alpha$). For details, see Bagaria (2023).

[32] The notions of *singleton, unordered pair*, and *Wiener–Kuratowski ordered pair* are explicitly definable: respectively, $\{x\} = z \leftrightarrow_{def} \forall y (y \in z \leftrightarrow y = x)$; $\{x, y\} = z \leftrightarrow_{def} \forall u (u \in z \leftrightarrow u = x \vee u = y)$; $(x, y) =_{def} \{\{x\}, \{x, y\}\}$.

stating that every nonempty set x contains an individual y sharing no elements with x;[33]

(Union) $\forall x \exists y \forall z(z \in y \leftrightarrow \exists u(z \in u \wedge u \in x))$,

stating that, for every set x of sets u, there is a set y containing the members of the members of x;[34]

(Powerset) $\forall x \exists y \forall z(z \in y \leftrightarrow z \subseteq x)$,

stating that, for every set x, there is a set y containing all the subsets of x, where the notion of *subset* is explicitly definable as $x \subseteq y \leftrightarrow_{def} \forall z(z \in x \rightarrow z \in y)$. The powerset y of x can be defined as: $\wp(x) = y \leftrightarrow_{def} \forall z(z \in y \leftrightarrow z \subseteq x)$;

(Infinity) $\exists x(\emptyset \in x \wedge \forall y(y \in x \rightarrow y \cup \{y\} \in x))$,

stating the existence of at least a set containing denumerably many members;[35]

(Replacement) $\forall u \exists! w \phi(u, w) \rightarrow \forall z \exists x \forall y(y \in x \leftrightarrow \exists w(w \in z \wedge \phi(w, y)))$,

stating that, if a formula ϕ relates each set u to a unique w, then starting from any set z in the hierarchy, another set x can be formed by replacing all members of z by other individuals according to ϕ;

(Choice) $\forall x(\forall y(y \in x \rightarrow \exists z(z \in y)) \wedge \forall y \forall z(y \in x \wedge z \in x \wedge y \neq z \rightarrow \neg \exists u(u \in z \wedge u \in y)) \rightarrow \exists w \forall y(y \in x \rightarrow \exists! z(z \in y \wedge z \in w)))$,

stating that, for every set x of pairwise-disjoint nonempty sets y, z, there exists a set w containing exactly one element from each set in x.

Possibly, the most renowned (consistent) AP interpreting at least some of ZFC is the restriction of BLV Boolos calls "New V" – see Boolos (1989, 1987b):

(New V) $\forall X \forall Y(\epsilon X = \epsilon Y \leftrightarrow ((Big(X) \wedge Big(Y)) \vee \forall x(Xx \leftrightarrow Yx)))$,

where *Big* is the property of concepts "being equinumerous with the universal concept $x = x$." Boolos's suggestion is based on the set-theoretic conception of the *limitation of size*, according to which in order to avoid contradiction, sets

---

[33] Foundation guarantees that no set is self-membered, since it prevents the existence of (infinite) loops of set membership in the cumulative hierarchy.

[34] The operation of union is explicitly definable: $\bigcup x = y \leftrightarrow_{def} \forall z(z \in y \leftrightarrow \exists u(z \in u \wedge u \in x))$, as well as the operation of union between sets: $x \cup y = z \leftrightarrow_{def} \forall u(u \in z \leftrightarrow u \in x \vee u \in y)$.

[35] With the axioms provided so far, ZFC interprets PA, by defining each natural number n as the set containing all natural numbers smaller than n: By defining $0 =_{def} \emptyset$ and $s(n) =_{def} n \cup \{n\}$ (the successor of n), we then define $1 =_{def} s(0) =_{def} \{\emptyset\}$; $2 =_{def} s(s(0)) =_{def} \{\emptyset, \{\emptyset\}\}$, and so on. There is exactly one set containing all and only the sets of such a progression, namely the set ω of all natural numbers.

in the set-theoretic universe cannot be too large. The limitation of size view, along with the iterative conception, is taken to be incorporated in ZFC.

The violation of the limitation of size constraint is provided as a possible explanation of set-theoretic paradoxes in Cantor's naïve set theory.[36] Besides Extensionality, the latter amounts to the axiom schema:

(Naïve Comprehension) $\exists x \forall y (y \in x \leftrightarrow \phi y) - \phi$ does not contain x free,

stating the existence of a set corresponding to any formula ϕ.

Naïve Comprehension is inconsistent. By plugging the condition $y = y$ in the right-hand side of Naïve Comprehension, there must exist the universal set $\mathcal{u}$, that is, the set containing every individual – *including itself*, since also $\mathcal{u}$ is self-identical. Now, recall Cantor's theorem: For any set x, the cardinality of its powerset $\wp(x)$ is larger than the cardinality of x. The theorem is proved by showing that there is no injective function mapping each subset of x to the elements of x. The universal set $\mathcal{u}$ will contain every set, including all of its subsets. Hence, $\mathcal{u}$ must contain enough elements for each of its subsets to be mapped into. If so, the cardinality of $\wp(\mathcal{u})$ cannot be larger than $\mathcal{u}$'s, which contradicts Cantor's theorem. So, the universal set $\mathcal{u}$ does not exist. This is the so-called *Cantor's paradox*.

The latter (as well as other paradoxes such as that of Russell, the Burali–Forti paradox concerning the nonexistence of the largest ordinal number, and the contradiction ensuing from the assumption of the existence of the largest cardinal number) is (at least partially) blamed on the fact that Naïve Comprehension allows for the existence of sets that are "too big," Limiting the size of the existing sets is one of the strategies (and philosophical underpinnings) of contemporary set theory.

Besides having models, Boolos's New V implies that "small" concepts have the same extension just in case they are co-extensional; but in case concepts X, Y are *Big*, their extensions are identical, even if X, Y are not co-extensional.[37] Interestingly, PA^2 and some amount of ZFC are derivable from New V. The notion of *set* can be explicitly defined in Boolos's setting:

(Set) $Set(x) \leftrightarrow_{def} \exists X(x = \epsilon X \land \neg Big(X))$,

meaning that x is a set just in case there's a concept X whose extension is x and X is small. Set membership can also be explicitly defined: $x \in y \leftrightarrow_{def} \exists X(y = \epsilon X \land Xx)$. By such definitions, New V proves Extensionality, Empty Set, Pairing, Separation, and Replacement. It also proves restricted versions

---

[36] See e.g. Hallett (1984).
[37] Note that Boolos calls New V-extensions *subtensions*.

of Union and Foundation.[38] New V entails neither Powerset nor Infinity. The latter result means that by New V and unrestricted SOL, it cannot be determined whether the concept of *being a natural number* is big. Finally, in general, New V and similar APs have very different models, that is, both well-founded and non-well-founded.[39]

Boolos's result falls short of interpreting all of ZFC in a consistent system of BLV. Cook (2003) proposes an extension of New V, starting from an AP for ordinal numbers, namely the *Size-Restricted Ordinal Abstraction Principle* (SOAP),[40] so that all of ZFC is interpretable in a consistent system of BLV.

Recently, an alternative view concerning APs that interprets set theory, that is, *dynamic abstraction* in Linnebo (2010, 2013, 2016, 2018), has been proposed. Its philosophical underpinning is as follows. Suppose APs are philosophically conceived of primarily as principles determining identity and distinctness facts about abstracts. If so, first-order quantification on the right-hand side of APs should presuppose the identity of the individuals it varies over, but those are exactly the objects APs are supposed to individuate in the first place. In this respect, such APs are *first-orderly impredicative* – see, for example, Linnebo (2016).

---

[38] In particular, Union restricted to *sets* is derivable from New V. Let a concept X be *closed* just in case all those sets whose members are X are X as well: $Closed(X) \leftrightarrow_{def} \forall y((Set(y) \wedge \forall z(z \in y \rightarrow Xz)) \rightarrow Xy)$. A set x is *pure* just in case it falls under all closed concepts (i.e. $\forall X(Closed(X) \rightarrow Xx)$) – in particular, $\emptyset$ will fall under all closed concepts, and so will its singleton, and the set containing $\emptyset$ and its singleton, and so on. If restricted to pure sets, Foundation is derivable from New V. See Boolos (1989).

[39] See Jané and Uzquiano (2004). For a further approach similar to Boolos's, see Shapiro (2003), where the property of being small is substituted by the property of *being good*, roughly to be read as "being a set." Also, for consistent restrictions of the right-hand side of BLV that moreover substitute the underlying (first-order) logic with a *free* logic, see Payne (2013a) and Conti (2020).

[40] Famously, set theory provides also a definition of *ordinal numbers* – see Bagaria (2023) and footnote 29. Abstractionist programs have investigated whether ordinals (and ordinal arithmetic) can be consistently recovered by abstraction. An unrestricted second-order AP engineered to introduce ordinals, e.g. $Ord(R) = Ord(S) \leftrightarrow R \simeq S$ stating that the ordinal number of a dyadic relation R is identical with the ordinal number of a dyadic relation S if, and only if, R and S are isomorphic, along with unrestricted SOL would yield the Burali–Forti paradox – see e.g. Hale (2020) and Rumfitt (2018). Different consistent restrictions on ordinal abstraction have been proposed – see e.g. Florio and Leach-Krouse (2017), Hale (2020), and Shapiro and Wright (2006). A further line of research in abstractionism worth mentioning is *structural abstractionism*, i.e. (formal) axiomatic systems of abstraction governing mathematical structures – a way to bring together some of the main orientations in the philosophy of mathematics of the past forty years, i.e. structuralism and abstractionism; for effective introductions to structuralism, see e.g. Hellman and Shapiro (2018) and Reck and Schiemer (2023). See e.g. Leach-Krouse (2015), Linnebo and Pettigrew (2014), Litland (2022), and Wigglesworth (2018). For further considerations on abstractionism and structuralism, see also Boccuni and Woods (2020), Doherty (2021), Reck (2021), Schiemer (2021), and Section 6.

Dummett (1991) argued that only first-orderly *predicative* APs do not presuppose that the objects introduced on the left are already available for quantification, and thus that there is philosophical motivation to prefer first-orderly predicative APs over first-orderly impredicative ones. However, predicative APs are typically mathematically weak.[41] According to Dummett, abstractionists are therefore left with the dilemma of choosing between mathematically fruitful but philosophically unsound *impredicative* abstraction, and philosophically motivated but mathematically dry *predicative* abstraction.

The aforementioned concern can motivate alternative conceptions of abstraction. In this regard, Linnebo (2010, 2013, 2016, 2018) provides the philosophical motivation and formal tools for such an alternative framework – which we will further investigate in Section 4: In Linnebo's dynamic abstraction, the individuation of BLV-extensions proceeds in stages (via stepwise extensions of the interpretation of first-order quantifiers), starting from an ontology of "old" objects, whose identities are already established and which the equivalence relation of BLV applies to, and providing individuation conditions for "new" objects (i.e. extensions) whose identity is dependent on the objects in the previous interpretation. In such a dynamic setting, predicative abstraction is *iterated* over larger and larger domains. On the one hand, this approach retains the philosophical motivation for first-order predicativity. On the other, it restores the mathematical strength of (predicative) APs.

The formal setting is constituted by a (modal) plural logic and a plural formulation of BLV. In this setting, the interaction between old and new objects is cashed out in terms of the modal operators $\Box\phi$ and $\Diamond\phi$ – which nevertheless are not conceived of as expressing metaphysical modality, but rather as "no matter how the domain of abstract objects is extended, it will remain the case that ϕ," and "the domain of abstract objects can be extended so that it is the case that ϕ," respectively. In order to spell out exactly how modality and abstraction interact, Linnebo factorizes abstraction in an existence principle and an extensionality principle. The former is

(Potential Collapse) $\Box\forall xx \Diamond \exists y(EXT(xx,y))$,

which postulates that, no matter how the domain is extended, for every plurality xx, the domain can be extended so that there is the extension of xx. Furthermore,

---

[41] For example, *Two-Sorted Hume's Principle* (HP2S) is as HP except that the cardinality function maps nonarithmetical concepts to arithmetical objects, where nonarithmetical objects and arithmetical objects belong to distinct sorts – see Linnebo (2016, p. 250). HP2S does not prove the successor axiom.

(Extensionality) $EXT(xx,x) \wedge EXT(yy,y) \rightarrow (x = y \leftrightarrow \Box \forall z(z < xx \leftrightarrow z < yy))$

posits that if x,y are the extensions of xx,yy respectively, they are identical just in case xx,yy are coextensive, no matter how the domain is extended. At the same time, the underlying plural logic is also modalized:

$$\Diamond \exists xx \Box \forall y(y < xx \leftrightarrow \phi^\Diamond y), \qquad (2.11)$$

where $\phi^\Diamond y$ is the "potentialist translation" of ϕ, that is, the result of replacing each ordinary quantifier in ϕ with the corresponding modalized quantifier. Still, given the background assumption that pluralities are modally rigid (pluralities cannot gain members and, if $x < xx$, then necessarily so), the modal plural comprehension axiom has to be restricted – hence, for example, the alleged plurality corresponding to the formula "$x = x$" would not be admitted since it would not be modally rigid, provided the expansion of the domain.[42] Notably, all (potentialist translations of) axioms of ZFC except Infinity and Replacement follow. For Infinity and Replacement to follow as well, further assumptions are needed.[43]

On the philosophical side, Linnebo's approach shares Aristotle's two fundamental insights in the philosophy of mathematics: First, the mathematical universe is never complete and it is always possible to individuate new mathematical objects (Linnebo and Shapiro 2017); second, these objects depend for their existence and their properties on nonmathematical entities – see Section 4.2.3.

2.7 Invariance

Famously, Frege conjectured BLV to be a logical principle.[44] After all, one of his main aims was to derive the basic laws of arithmetic from logic and definitions alone. Of course, given Russell's paradox, BLV is not logical at all. But the mere consistency of an AP is not sufficient for its logicality: Even consistent APs such as, for example, HP seem hardly logical, since they may imply the existence of denumerably many individuals.[45]

---

[42] Note that, depending on the kind of higher-order entities involved in APs, whether intensional or extensional, e.g. concepts or pluralities, restrictions might be applied in different ways. Pluralities may be required to be modally constrained, whereas concepts, being intensional entities, are rather hard to capture modally. For instance, unlike what happens with pluralities, it seems rather reasonable to postulate the existence of the concept corresponding to "$x = x$." Hence, restrictions must rather apply to which extensions exist. See e.g. Linnebo (2009a, 2010, 2018).

[43] For further details, see e.g. Linnebo (2018, chapter 12). For a different approach to dynamic abstraction than Linnebo's, see Studd (2016).

[44] To be fair, he did with reservations: see Frege (1893/1903, *Foreword*, p. VII).

[45] See e.g. Boolos (1987a, p. 199).

What the logicality criteria are supposed to be is a complex issue.[46] Still, there's agreement that one of the (necessary) conditions for logicality is *topic neutrality*:

> [a] logical principle is valid in any kind of discourse, no matter what kind of objects this discourse is concerned with.[47]

Topic neutrality is often formally cashed out in terms of *invariance under permutations* of the logical expressions, namely their insensitivity to the particular identities of the objects they vary over – where, generally, a permutation π is a one-one function mapping a domain onto itself.[48]

Starting from Fine (2002), the notion of invariance has been investigated as concerns APs. As Antonelli (2010b) points out, there are three senses in which invariance may be investigated in this respect: the invariance of the abstraction operator; the invariance of the equivalence relation; the invariance of the overall principle. There are very few invariant abstraction operators, and they are rather uninteresting mathematically. Furthermore, the invariance of the overall AP follows from the invariance of its equivalence relation; therefore, Antonelli (2010b) focuses on the latter: Given a relation R on a second-order domain that is closed under permutations,

(1) R is *internally invariant* if, and only if, for any permutation π, $R(X, Y)$ if, and only if, $R(\pi[X], \pi[Y])$;
(2) R is *doubly invariant* if, for any pair π_1, π_2 of permutations, $R(X, Y)$ if, and only if, $R(\pi_1[X], \pi_2[Y])$;
(3) R is *(simply) invariant* if, and only if, $R(X, \pi[X])$ holds for any permutation π.

Double and simple invariance are logically equivalent; simple invariance implies internal invariance.

The equinumerosity relation appearing on the right-hand side of HP is simply invariant. According to Antonelli (2010b), what the simple invariance of equinumerosity shows is that the very notion of cardinality can be deemed logical by those supporting the view that invariance is a necessary condition for logicality, or at the very least the invariance of equinumerosity can play a role in the acceptability of APs (e.g. Fine 2002) and thus in the debate on the so-called *Bad Company problem* – see Section 2.8. The alleged logicality of equinumerosity does not imply the logical nature of cardinal numbers. In this

---

[46] For a survey, see Linnebo (2022, section 3).
[47] Linnebo (2022).
[48] See MacFarlane (2017, section 5) for a survey.

sense, the logicality of cardinality supports a *deflationist* view of cardinal numbers: Since HP is (simply) invariant, it is insensitive to the underlying nature of the objects in the domains it permutes over; so "[a]nything at all – even ordinary objects – can play the role of these *abstracta*, as long as the choice respects the equivalence relation."[49] Later, Cook (2017) refines the notions of invariance presented in Antonelli (2010b) and Fine (2002) by investigating *doubly internal invariance*,[50] and shows that HP is the most fine-grained AP satisfying it.[51]

Neologicists claim that HP is *analytic* albeit not a logical truth. In §3 of *Grundlagen*, Frege famously claims that a sentence is analytic if "in carrying out [its proof] we come only on general logical laws and definitions." Frege's notion of analyticity must be distinguished from Kant's, according to which a judgment is analytic if the predicate is already contained in the subject.

These two senses of analyticity must moreover be distinguished from the contemporary notions of metaphysical and epistemic analyticity (Boghossian 1996):

- a statement is metaphysically analytic if it is true purely in virtue of the meaning of some of its component expressions;
- a statement is epistemically analytic if grasping its meaning is sufficient to have a justified belief that the content expressed by that statement is true.

Hale and Wright (2001a) claim that even though HP is analytic neither in Kant's nor in Frege's sense,[52] it can still be deemed analytic in the sense that it is "determinative of the concept it thereby serves to explain" (p. 14).

It is worth noting that a statement can be analytic in Hale and Wright's sense without being metaphysically or epistemically analytic. In particular, a statement can be analytic in the Neologicist sense (that is, the implicit definition of a concept) without being metaphysically analytic (that is, true in virtue of meaning).

---

[49] Antonelli (2010b, p. 290). A further notion of invariance, inspired by Antonelli (2010b), is presented in Woods (2014) and Boccuni and Woods (2020), which is weaker than full-fledged invariance, but it applies to the abstraction operator of HP – see also footnote 92 and Section 6.

[50] An equivalence relation $E(X, Y)$ is doubly internally invariant if, and only if, for any model $M = < \Delta, I >$ and one-one mappings $f_1, f_2, f_1 : X \to \Delta$ and $f_2 : Y \to \Delta$, $E(X, Y)$ if, and only if, $E(f_1[X], f_2[Y])$. Doubly internal invariance implies both double and internal invariance.

[51] Notably, requiring that APs's equivalence relations be "doubly invariant corresponds to one (weak) way of requiring that APs fully fix the structure of the abstracts that they introduce" (Cook 2017, p. 21), where the latter feature is called *relative categoricity* in Walsh and Ebels-Duggan (2015).

[52] Note that HP does not provide an explicit definition of the cardinality operator. Moreover, HP does not have a subject-predicate form; therefore, it cannot be analytic in Kant's sense.

Hale and Wright (2000) argue that HP is epistemically analytic, that is, can be known a priori (see Section 5.3). Neologicists claim moreover that PA^2 is analytic in Frege's sense, that is, its axioms can be derived by an implicit definition and SOL (see Section 5.3.2). In the most recent iterations of the abstractionist program, analyticity has been dropped (Linnebo 2018, p. 3) even though the claim that APs can provide implicit definitions is retained (Rayo 2013, p. 187; Linnebo 2018, p. xiii).

2.8 The Bad Company Problem

Many APs, even those that are consistent, are unacceptable because they are incompatible with other principles with the same form (Dummett 1991, 1998; Boolos 1998a; Weir 2003).[53]

An example is Wright's (1998) *Nuisance Principle* (NP), which states that two concepts have the same "nuisance" if their difference is finite:[54]

(NP) $(\forall X)(\forall Y)(v(X) = v(Y) \leftrightarrow (\mathrm{Fin}(X \wedge \neg Y) \wedge \mathrm{Fin}(\neg X \wedge Y)))$.

NP has only finite models. Therefore, it cannot be satisfied jointly with HP, which, to the contrary, has models that are at least denumerable.[55] As remarked by Linnebo (2009b, p. 324), "attractive principles like Hume's Principle are surrounded by bad companions." The *Bad Company problem* consists in sorting out acceptable principles from unacceptable ones.

Unacceptable principles seem easy to come by. Many pairwise inconsistent abstractions take the form of "Distraction principles" (Weir 2003, p. 17), namely, APs whose abstraction function behaves like the function characterized by BLV unless both X and Y satisfy some second-order formula Φ:

(D) $(\forall X)(\forall Y)(\sigma(X) = \sigma(Y) \leftrightarrow ((\Phi(X) \wedge \Phi(Y)) \vee \forall x(Xx \leftrightarrow Yy)))$.

At the same time, New V and other mathematically promising principles are instances of (D). The problem consists in selecting all and only the acceptable Distractions while leaving out the principles that are incompatible with them.

Over the years, several authors have formulated a plethora of increasingly strong criteria for acceptable abstraction (cf. e.g. Cook (2021a, 2021b),

---

[53] By "same form," we mean second-order APs such that the equivalence relation on their right can be defined in pure SOL.

[54] NP is a modification of Boolos's (1989) *Parity*, which assigns the same "parity" to two concepts if, and only if, they differ evenly and finitely.

[55] Ebels-Duggan (2015) shows that NP is inconsistent with HP, given minimal assumptions about infinite concepts.

and Cook and Linnebo (2018) for recent overviews of the criteria and their rationale). Here, we will simply list the main ones.

Criterion 1 (Consistency) *An AP is acceptable only if it is consistent (CON).*

Criterion 2 (Unboundedness) *An AP is acceptable only if it is unbound (UNB), that is, for any cardinal γ there is some cardinal $\kappa \geq \gamma$ s.t. AP is κ-satisfiable, that is, satisfiable in a model of cardinality κ.*

Criterion 3 (Semantic Field-Conservativeness) *An AP is acceptable only if it is semantically Field-conservative (FCON), that is, for any theory T to which AP can be consistently added and for any sentence ϕ:*

$$\{T + AP\} \models \phi^{\neg @} \text{ only if } T \models \phi,$$

where $\phi^{\neg @}$ is the result of restricting the quantifiers of ϕ to objects that satisfy the formula $\neg \exists F (x = \Sigma_{AP}(F))$, that is, are not abstracts of AP.[56]

Criterion 4 (Irenicity) *An AP is acceptable only if it is irenic (IRN), that is, only if AP is (i) Field-conservative, and (ii) compatible with any other Field-conservative APs.*

Criterion 5 (Strong Stability) *An AP is acceptable only if it is strongly stable (SSTB), that is, there is a cardinal k such that AP is γ-satisfiable if, and only if, $\gamma \geq \kappa$.*

The mutual relations between UNB, FCON, IRN, and SSTB are proved in Cook and Linnebo (2018). Cook and Linnebo also argue that a solution to the Bad Company problem requires the combination of strong stability with two other criteria:

Criterion 6 (Heck Stability) *An AP is acceptable only if it is Heck-stable (HSTB), that is, (i) strongly stable and (ii) critically full. AP is critically full if for each critical point κ of AP, any model of AP of size κ contains κ abstracts of the sort characterized by AP. κ is a critical point of AP if AP is κ-satisfiable and there is some $\gamma < \kappa$ s.t. AP is not λ-satisfiable for any $\lambda \leq \gamma < \kappa$.*

---

[56] HP is not, however, *deductively* conservative over SOL. Mackereth and Avigad (2022) show that Heck's (1997b) two-sorted HP – which is as HP except that the cardinality function maps nonarithmetical concepts to arithmetical objects – is not deductively conservative either. This gives further reasons to understand the relevant notion of conservativeness semantically; see also Mackereth (in press) for a discussion of the philosophical significance of this result.

Criterion 7 (Monotonicity) *An AP is acceptable only if it is monotonic (MONO), that is, its equivalence relation Eq is intrinsic, that is, for any X and Y,*

$$Eq(F, G) \; \textit{iff} \; Eq^{F \cup G}(F, G),$$

where $Eq^{F \cup G}$ is the result of restricting all the quantifiers of Eq to objects that fall under either X or Y.

The relations among combinations of SSTB, HSTB, and MONO are proved in Cook (2021b). Both Fine (2005) and Cook (2017) explore invariance as a condition on acceptable abstraction.

The Bad Company problem gets worse, however, when we consider the mathematical strength of acceptable APs: The APs that would be most suited for recovering mathematical theories other than arithmetic are often unacceptable. An example is George Boolos's New V. New V is sufficient to recover a remarkable portion of ZFC; however, it is not conservative, since it implies that the universe is well-ordered (Shapiro and Weir 2000, pp. 304–309). In general, Uzquiano (2009) shows that no AP that complies with SSTB can recover ZFC. As noted by Studd (2016, pp. 595–596), philosophical abstractionism seems to face a dilemma: Either the criteria introduced are permissive enough to include promising cases of abstraction such as New V, but, then, the Bad Company problem resurfaces, or those criteria are restrictive enough to avoid it, but, then, New V and other promising principles are ruled out.

3 Philosophical Abstractionism I: Semantics

3.1 Introduction

According to Frege and Scottish Neologicists (Section 2.4), expressions of the form "#X" are singular terms. There is no general agreement, however, on whether expressions appearing on the left-hand side of APs are indeed such. These considerations often rely on the analysis of natural language. For instance, in the natural language, number words like, for example, "four" can take on different roles. In this section, we will focus particularly on numerical expressions, since most of the relevant literature concerns number words. Specifically, we will survey the main positions concerning their semantic role: the *substantival* view, ascribing singulartermhood to number words (Frege; Scottish Neologicism; Rayo; Linnebo – Section 3.2); the *adjectival* reading, which regards number words as modifiers of nouns (Hofweber; Moltmann – Section 3.3.1); the *quantificational* perspective, conceiving of number words as numerical quantifiers (Hodes – Section 3.3.2). Other things being equal, similar considerations may apply to expressions of the form "$\Sigma\alpha$" appearing on the left-hand side of APs in a more general abstractionist perspective.

3.2 The Substantival View

Consider the following statement:

(1) Jupiter has four moons.

Statement (1) can be provided with a reading that Frege subscribed to and Dummett (1991, p. 99) calls *substantival*. According to this reading, (1) can be paraphrased as

(2) The number of Jupiter's moons is four,

whose logical form is that of an *identity statement* between the referent of the singular term "the number of Jupiter's moons" and the referent of the singular term "four."[57]

It is fair to say that Frege's reading of expressions of the form "the number of Jupiter's moons," "4," and more in general abstract terms of the form "$\Sigma\alpha$" is tightly connected to his view concerning the basic logical categories of *function* and *argument* – see, for example, Frege (1879, 1891, 1893/1903), and Cook (2023) for an overview.

In Frege's intentions, a logically perfect language, like the one exposed in Frege (1879, 1893/1903), was to be devoted to several aims, among which was formulating the axioms and inference rules of logic, in order to provide explicit definitions of the mathematical notions necessary to derive the basic laws of arithmetic from logical principles and definitions alone – as well as the basic laws of real and, possibly, complex analysis. At its core, such a language relied on the fundamental logical distinction between function and argument, with which Frege replaced Aristotle's dichotomy between subject and predicate in the logical analysis of language.

Slightly oversimplifying, we can take Frege's functions to be denoted by predicates with at least a free variable (in a contemporary notation), and Frege's arguments to be placeholders for names of objects (e.g. individual constants in contemporary formal logic). According to Frege, a function is "unsaturated"

---

[57] The substantival reading is connected with the so-called *easy argument for Platonism*: Consider the identity statement (2); (2) is true; therefore numbers exist. This argument is usually rejected by the supporters of the adjectival strategy: see e.g. Felka (2014), Hofweber (2005), Knowles (2015), Moltmann (2013, 2016), and Snyder (2017). See also Section 4.1.

(i.e. it has to take names as arguments in order to have a (truth-)value), whereas names of objects are "saturated" (i.e. nothing is required for them to have values, if any). Therefore, when asking what logical categories expressions in

(3) $2 + 3 = 5$

belong to, and considering the expression "2," either "2" stands for a function that has to be saturated in order to have a value, or no saturation is needed at all. Both logico-linguistic analysis and cautionary anti-empiricist views (such as J. S. Mill's, which Frege disputed in e.g. Frege 1884) prompted Frege to argue that "2" is a name of a (self-subsistent) object.

In this respect, Frege's substantival reading of (1) as (2) is coherent both with his distinction between function and argument, and his view of numbers as objects. Given his foundational aims, equations like (3) were of the utmost importance to Frege, and his substantival reading accounts for them: The logical form of (3) consists in the application of a function symbol ("+") to two singular terms ("2" and "3"), so that the number "2 + 3" denotes is the same number (=) as the number denoted by "5."

Since number words (and numerals) are singular terms standing for self-subsistent (abstract) objects (i.e. the numbers), and since we have no direct access to abstract objects, an issue may arise as to how the reference of number words (and numerals) is fixed. In this respect, Frege attributes a crucial role to his *Context Principle*, which cautions, against psychologistic inclinations, to "never ask for the meaning of a word in isolation, but only in the context of a proposition."[58] Particularly relevant to the aim of reference fixing of number words in general are identity statements like (2) and (3). Still, as Frege (1884, §62) famously points out:

> [i]f we are to use a symbol a to signify an object, we must have a criterion
> for deciding in all cases whether b is the same as a ....

In particular, the meaning of identities such as (2) has to be established, with no use of the expressions "the number of Jupiter's moons" or "four" at all. Therefore,

> [w]hen we have thus acquired a means of arriving at a determinate number
> and of recognizing it again as the same, we can assign it a number word as
> its proper name.[59]

In this respect, the truth-conditions of an AP for numbers (and Fregean abstract objects in general) are expected to deliver contextually the reference

---

[58] Frege (1884, p. xxii).
[59] *Ibidem.*

of the singular terms on its left-hand side.[60] At this point, Frege discusses what later would be known as HP, if only to discard it because of the so-called *Caesar Problem*,[61] and provide an explicit definition of numbers as equivalence classes closed under the equinumerosity relation – which was doomed to failure due to Russell's paradox.[62]

In a rather Fregean vein, Wright (1983) and Hale and Wright (2001a) rely on the Context Principle in order to bestow meaning upon expressions like "$\#X$." In particular, in Hale and Wright's view, the proposition supposed to contextually fix the reference of "$\#X$" is HP.

That is not enough, though, to guarantee that expressions like "$\#X$" are indeed singular terms to begin with. In order to establish this, Scottish Neologicists rely on several claims.

First, they propose syntactic criteria to distinguish singular terms from other expressions. In particular, those criteria amount to an *inferential test* and an *Aristotelian test*, both tracing back to Dummett (1973), according to which genuine singular terms display different inferential behavior than other expressions (especially, quantifiers), and singular terms, unlike predicates, have no contradictory expressions (i.e. it makes no sense to use "not (Mary)" in a sentence, but it does to use "not (smart)"), respectively.[63]

Second, once these criteria are in place, Scottish Neologicists rely on the *Syntactic Priority Thesis* (SPT) and HP. According to SPT, the truth of claims

---

[60] Dummett (1991) and Picardi (2017) highlight a tension between the role Frege attributes to the Context Principle and compositionality, in particular concerning APs, since compositionality requires that the truth-conditions of an AP are provided on the basis of the meaning of its relevant components. One way to solve this tension is to provide the truth-conditions of more complex sentences compositionally on the basis of atomic ones: crucially, identity statements – where the truth-conditions of the latter are provided by the Context Principle. As Picardi (2017) points out, compositionality delivers a *robust* notion of reference, which is particularly apt for Frege (1893/1903): "$\Sigma\alpha$" genuinely refers to an (abstract) object. As we'll see in what follows, this robust notion of reference is also openly ascribed to Scottish Neologicism by Dummett (1991, chapters 15–16) – see e.g. Wright (1983) and Hale and Wright (2001a). In particular, Dummett disputes that the referentiality of "$\Sigma\alpha$" is genuine, i.e. robust – in his words, "operative." Rather, he argues that the referentiality of abstract terms is *semantically idle* (or *thin*), since APs provide no identifying knowledge of what kind of objects "$\Sigma\alpha$" purportedly refers to. Dummett (1991), finally, contrasts the robust view of reference, which is proper of Platonism, with an austere view (proper of the intolerant reductionist, who denies that "$\Sigma\alpha$" is a singular term at all), and an intermediate view (proper of the tolerant reductionist, who agrees with the Platonist that "$\Sigma\alpha$" is indeed a singular term but denies that such a notion of reference is to be understood realistically). See e.g. Rayo (2013) for a more recent rendition of Dummett's and Picardi's solution.

[61] The Caesar Problem amounts to HP's incapability of establishing the truth-value of "mixed" identity statements like, e.g. "Caesar = 4." See Frege (1884, §§63–66), and Section 3.4.

[62] See Frege (1884, §68), and Section 2.3.

[63] See e.g. Dummett (1973, pp. 54–58, 174–179), Hale (2001b, 2001c) and Wright (1983, pp. 14, 24–25). For criticisms, see e.g. Schwartzkopff (2016), Wetzel (1990), and Rumfitt (2003).

involving numerical terms in singular term position suffices to guarantee that they refer to objects. Hence, since HP contains expressions of the form "$\#X$" that are singular terms by the syntactic criteria aforementioned and because they appear in singular term position (e.g. they flank the identity symbol), its truth is sufficient to justify the attribution of objectual reference to the singular terms on its left-hand side.

Precisely, by its surface syntax and the criteria for singulartermhood, "$\#X$" is indeed a singular term. Moreover, the right-hand side of HP is a truth of pure SOL (see Definition 2.4 in Section 2.4). Since HP is a material biconditional, from the truth of HP and its right-hand side, the identity statements on its left-hand side are also true. Since the latter are true claims containing numerical terms in singular term position, those terms are singular terms that do refer to objects (SPT).[64]

A similar reliance on the syntactic role of abstract terms and their appearance in (atomic) true sentences for their referentiality to be secured is in Rayo's (2013) *compositionalism*. Consider an uninterpreted first-order language L, and the assignment of truth-conditions to L's sentences. Of course, such an assignment has to satisfy logical entailment,[65] but otherwise we can pick *any* assignment. According to compositionalism, if the sentences of L are interpreted in this way, for a singular term t of L to be referential (i.e. to refer to an object in the world), all that is needed is that the world satisfies "the truth-conditions that were assigned to $\ulcorner\exists x(x = t)\urcorner$ (or some inferential analogue)."[66]

Linnebo (2018) labels both the Neologicist metasemantic view of reference fixing and Rayo's compositionalism *ultra-thin conceptions*, by which in general "an expression refers provided that, first, it has all the appropriate syntactic and inferential characteristics of a singular term, and second, the expression figures in appropriate true sentences."[67] He then contrasts both views with his *thin conception*, according to which, for the reference of (singular) abstract terms such as "$\Sigma\alpha$" to be fixed, APs as *identity criteria* for appropriate kinds of objects

---

[64] See also Section 4.2. Fine (2002) relies on Frege's Context Principle to support a view of abstraction establishing, rather than presupposing, the existence of the abstract objects governed by APs. Scottish Neologicists argue for a Platonic view of the objects governed by HP; to the contrary, Fine argues for a "creative" account of abstraction according to which, by relying on the Context Principle, "the objects are introduced into the discourse simultaneously with their assignments to the terms" (Fine 2002, p. 56).

[65] Rayo spells out logical entailment as follows: "if ψ is a logical consequence of ϕ, then the truth-conditions assigned to ϕ must demand at least as much of the world as the truth-conditions assigned to ψ" (Rayo 2014, footnote 1; see also Rayo 2013).

[66] Rayo (2014, pp. 498–499).

[67] Linnebo (2018, p. 123).

are sufficient. The process of reference fixing proceeds in stages. We start from a domain of "old" objects, reference to which is already accomplished. Then, an AP is introduced: Its right-hand side contains first-order quantifiers restricted to the old objects; and singular terms on its left-hand side refer to "new" objects.[68] Reference to the latter is accomplished via identity and distinctness facts based on an old ontology of individuals – which Linnebo (2018, p. 141) labels *semantic nonreductionism*.[69,70]

3.3 Nonsubstantival Views

In this section, we will present two main alternatives to the substantival view: the view by which (most) number words are adjectives, and consequently stand for a varied landscape of higher-order entities (Section 3.3.1); and the view according to which number words are quantificational expressions (Section 3.3.2).

3.3.1 The Adjectival View

The adjectival view interprets statements like (1) in Section 3.2 as capturing the primary usage of number words in natural language as *adjectives* – or *determiners*, namely expressions that modify nouns. On this reading, in (1) "four" appears in adjectival position as a modifier of "moons." In particular, "four" stands for a numerical property predicated of the semantic value of "moons" – the latter being a plurality or a property. Several authors subscribe to this view, though with crucial differences.

According to Hofweber (2005), (most occurrences of) number words in natural language are determiners, which have semantic values (i.e. properties) contributing to the truth-conditions of the statements in which they occur, but are not referential (in the way singular terms are, if at all). A clear example of this is statement (1).[71]

---

[68] This strategy is connected with the worry concerning first-order impredicativity of APs mentioned towards the end of Section 2.6.

[69] For further details, see in particular Section 4.2.3 and Linnebo (2018, chapter 8).

[70] In the views aforementioned, authors may diverge on how referentiality of singular terms is secured, but they in general agree that the referentiality at stake is genuine, i.e. "$\Sigma\alpha$" refers to a particular object, if any. But authors who agree on the genuine referentiality of "$\Sigma\alpha$" might disagree on the kind of reference involved: see Section 3.4 and footnote 92.

[71] The only exception Hofweber's proposal does not account for are statements of the form "Two is a prime number." See e.g. Hofweber (2005, p. 210). Hofweber contrasts the adjectival reading of statements like (1) with the substantival reading (which, to recall, conceive of "four" as a noun). In general, adjectives and nouns in natural language are not intersubstitutable, if grammaticality is to be preserved. So, e.g. "four" cannot belong to different syntactic (and

In Hofweber (2005), number words can be treated as determiners even in statements in which the nouns they modify do not occur explicitly, like e.g. "After dinner, I will have one, too," and in statements in which number words are not supposed to modify any noun, such as e.g. "Two are more than none." In these cases, number words are *bare* determiners.

Admittedly, this view is not straightforwardly applicable to genuinely arithmetical statements such as (3). In order to accommodate those kinds of statements also, according to Hofweber (2005, p. 195), we have to consider how "arithmetical symbols are first introduced to us and what meaning is given to them." Children have to accomplish several tasks when they learn basic arithmetic, among which are: learning number words and putting them in the right order; using them to count collections of things; mastering formal symbols such as Arabic numerals, and symbols for arithmetical operations. This seems to indicate that basic arithmetical statements like (3) are first learnt in one of their most ordinary uses, that is, counting things in collections. In this sense, "2," "3," and "5" are (bare) determiners that in time were abstracted away from simple operations of counting collections of ordinary things. As arithmetic gets more and more complex, cognitive difficulties kick in. In order to minimize them, we operate a process of *cognitive type coercion*: "[i]n reasoning our minds favor representations . . . about objects" (Hofweber 2005, p. 200). In order to simplify the task of understanding and calculating (more and more complex) arithmetical equations, a cognitive shift takes place from the type of (3), in which "2," "3," and "5" are bare determiners, to the type in which "2," "3," and "5" stand for objects of sorts.

This view does not straightforwardly account for statements such as (2), but according to Hofweber (2005, p. 210), in order to understand the relationship between statements (1) and (2), we have to consider their usage in communication. In particular, the difference between them is that (1) seems a subject-predicate sentence, whereas (2) seems to be a so-called *clefted* or *specificational* sentence, in which, unlike (1), information is *not* communicated neutrally but is conveyed via (2)'s *structural focus*. Still, it can be argued that the change in focus does not impact which syntactic category "four" belongs to. For instance, as Hofweber (2005) but also, for example, Moltmann (2013) and Felka (2014) argue, it would be odd to answer a question like "How many moons has Jupiter?" by (2): We'd rather expect the answer to come in the form

---

semantic) categories – therefore, its referent, if any, cannot belong to different ontological categories. Which is the primary reading of "four," the adjectival or the substantival one? This is what Hofweber (2005, 2023) calls *Frege's other puzzle*.

of (1) – or something along its lines.[72] So, in (2), "four" is a determiner that has been moved to a different syntactic position for communication purposes via structural focus.[73]

Other authors follow Hofweber's (2005) strategy, but with significant differences. For instance, on the basis of linguistic evidence, Moltmann (2013, 2016) proposes to divide the semantic role of number words in natural language in three categories. While subscribing to Hofweber's adjectival view as for numerals like "four" (even though numerals may behave syntactically like nouns), Moltmann argues that, on the one hand, prima facie singular terms such as "the number of Jupiter's moons" are not singular terms at all, but rather referential expressions standing for *number tropes*, that is, instantiated numerical properties ("the number of") of pluralities ("Jupiter's moons").[74] On the other hand, genuine numerical singular terms like "the number four" do refer to numbers as objects, and their genuine referentiality as full-fledged singular terms is brought about by the application of the function *number* to the determiner "four."[75]

3.3.2 The Quantificational View

Consider a consistent AP. Generally, the models of AP must contain at least as many individuals as needed in order to satisfy it. But those individuals need not be the one and only AP-objects – for example, cardinal numbers with respect to HP. For that matter, even models containing at least the appropriate cardinality of copies of Caesar can satisfy AP – provided the model is structured in the right way (e.g. as for HP, its models have to satisfy, e.g. the predecessor relation). Still, if reference of singular terms like "$\Sigma\alpha$" permutes over domains (modulo APs being satisfied), then it is indeterminate which particular objects AP-terms refer to. Therefore, it might be questioned that AP-terms are singular terms at all. This is the so-called *permutation argument*, which, as far as HP

---

[72] This argument relies on the so-called *question-answer analysis*. See e.g. Hofweber (2005), Knowles (2015), Moltmann (2013, 2016), and Snyder (2017). For a sympathetic although critical approach to such an analysis, see e.g. Felka (2014).

[73] For a recent debate on Hofweber's view, see e.g. Hofweber (2023), and Snyder, Samuels, and Shapiro (2022a, 2022b). For a critical view of (2) as a specificational sentence, in particular in Moltmann (2013), see Schwartzkopff (2015).

[74] See e.g. Snyder (2017) for an alternative view treating "the number of Jupiter's moons" as an individual concept.

[75] The genuine referentiality of numerical singular terms does not imply the existence of numbers as Platonic objects, though. Any nominalistic inclination can be accommodated via a fictionalist view of mathematical objects, Moltmann (2013) argues. For fictionalist accounts of mathematics, see e.g. Field (1980) and Yablo (2001, 2005).

is concerned, can be used to propose yet another possible reading of number words.[76]

Whereas the adjectival strategy relies on linguistic data, giving priority to natural language over formal languages for arithmetic, Hodes (1984, 1990) takes a hint from Frege's well-known examples in Frege (1884) on the number of Jupiter's moons, in order to revert to formal theories of arithmetic, and provide the logical form of Fregean alleged identity statements like (2) in terms of *numerical quantifiers*.

Hodes's analysis is prompted by the rejection of what he calls the *mathematical-object theory*, according to which, in short, numerical terms are object-designating singular terms. Hodes (1984, 1990) highlights some issues the mathematical-object theorist must address. In a nutshell, the mathematical-object theorist must provide an adequate answer to the issue concerning the "microstructure of reference to, e.g., cardinal numbers."[77] But here is the hitch. In clear-cut cases of referential efficacy to medium-sized objects, as well as natural and artificial kinds and even theoretical entities like positrons, causal relations seem to be problematically crucial. Such a philosophical difficulty becomes even more severe in the case of abstract, causally inert objects such as cardinal numbers, since as for the latter the kind of reference required seems to be "so pure, so unsustained by the cement of the universe, that reference to them and their ilk seems quite *sui generis*."[78]

Here is where Frege may come unwillingly to the rescue. Consider again statement (1). Even if just to discard it, Frege entertained briefly the possibility that its logical form is along the following lines:[79]

(4) There are exactly four moons of Jupiter.

In Hodes's view, though, the "linguistic apparatus of a branch of mathematics is a package built to allow certain higher-order statements to be encoded 'down' into a more familiar and tractable first-order form."[80] So, instead of reading statement (2) as the logical form of (4), as Frege suggested, Hodes proceeds the other way around: Identity statements between the referents (objects) of singular terms like (2) really are *quantificational* statements like (4), whose demi-formal form is

---

[76] See Assadian (2019) for the permutation argument as applied to HP specifically.

[77] Hodes (1984, p. 126).

[78] Hodes (1984, p. 127).

[79] See e.g. Frege (1884, §55) and Dummett (1991, chapter 9). Precisely, in Frege (1884, §55), a definition of individual numbers in terms of what we now call (first-order) numerical quantifiers is investigated.

[80] Hodes (1990, p. 237).

(5) $\exists_4 x(x$ is a moon of Jupiter),

where $\exists_4$ is a first-orderly definable *numerical quantifier*,[81] and "4" is syncategorematic, that is, it is not referential.

On the basis of the latter analysis, then, numbers can be obtained as objects. In particular, a *numberer* is a higher-order function taking concepts as arguments and having objects as values: The standard numberer (i.e. "the number of") assigns to a concept the number of objects falling under that concept. A *representor* is a higher-order function taking numerical objects-quantifiers to objects.[82] The standard representor assigns a numerical quantifier to a "special sort of object intrinsically, internally, and just plain *specially* related to that quantifier."[83] These special objects are the numbers: a number is "an object that canonically represents a cardinality quantifier," and it is "the nature of a cardinal number to be intimately related to a particular cardinality object-quantifier."[84] For instance, the number 4 is an object whose nature consists in its representing the numerical quantifier $\exists_4$.[85] Thus, the logical form of statement (2) is a statement about numerical quantifiers: "what appears to be a first-order theory about objects of a distinctive sort really is an encoding of a fragment of third-order logic,"[86] which is first-orderized for the sake of mathematical tractability.

This view of mathematical discourse supports Hodes's *coding fictionalism*: Whenever a number term is used as in, for example, (2), we pretend to posit objects that represent numerical quantifiers, for example, $\exists_4$. In this respect, numbers are "fictions 'created' with a special purpose, to encode numerical object-quantifiers and thereby enable us to 'pull down' a fragment of third-order logic, dressing it in first-order clothing."[87]

3.4 The Caesar Problem

As mentioned in Section 3.2, Frege discarded HP as a contextual definition of the natural numbers because of the so-called *Caesar Problem* (CP). In §67,

---

[81] Finite (first-order) numerical quantifiers are easily definable in the language of FOL. For instance, $\exists_4 x(\phi x) \leftrightarrow_{def} \exists x, y, z, w(\phi x \wedge \phi y \wedge \phi z \wedge \phi w \wedge x \neq y \neq z \neq w \wedge \forall v(\phi v \rightarrow x = v \vee y = v \vee z = v \vee w = v))$.

[82] A numberer is paired with a representor if, and only if, the numberer assigns to all concepts falling under a given numerical quantifier what the representor assigns to that quantifier.

[83] Hodes (1984, p. 133).

[84] Hodes (1984, p. 139).

[85] Hodes's proposal interprets PA, but it does so in a *third*-order logic, since "the number of" contains a free variable ranging over numberers, in order to retain generality. Rayo (2002) shows that the same result can be achieved in a *second*-order logic.

[86] Hodes (1984, p. 143).

[87] Hodes (1984, p. 144).

Frege quickly raises an objection to his own attempt to define directions using an AP:

> Th[e definition] does not provide for all cases. It will not, for instance, decide for us whether England is the same as the direction of the Earth's axis . . . . Naturally no one is going to confuse England with the direction of Earth's axis; but that is no thanks to our definition of direction.[88]

HP is similarly incapable of establishing the truth-value of statements like, for example, "Caesar $= \#X$."[89]

CP generalizes over APs. As Cook and Ebert (2005, p. 122) point out, APs "fix the truth conditions for identity statements regarding abstracts (i.e. the truth conditions of the identity on the left-hand side of the abstraction principle) in virtue of the equivalence relation on the right-hand side." However, generally APs stay silent as for the truth-conditions of "mixed" identity statements of the form

$$\Sigma\alpha = q, \tag{3.1}$$

where "q" is not a term of the form "$\Sigma\alpha$."[90]

CP is particularly worrisome for Neologicism. If CP is not solved, Neologicists cannot argue that HP's truth contextually bestows reference upon number-terms appearing on its left-hand side, and therefore, by SPT and the

---

[88] Frege (1884, §66).

[89] It has been debated what kind of problem CP really is – ontological, semantic, or epistemological. See e.g. Blanchette (2021), Heck (2011a), and Schirn (2002) as for CP in Frege, and MacBride (2006) as for CP in Neologicism. Regardless, we will examine it in this section, because CP affects the issue of reference in Neologicism, and, generally, the issue of the truth-conditions of identity statements involving AP-terms. However, we will resume it in Section 4.3, since at least some authors have proposed solutions to CP that enhance the underlying metaphysics.

[90] As a special case of CP, Cook and Ebert (2005) investigate what they call the *cross-sortal identification problem* (C-R Problem) – C for "complex numbers" and R for "reals." Given any two APs,

$$\Sigma_{Eq_1}(\alpha) = \Sigma_{Eq_1}(\beta) \leftrightarrow Eq_1(\alpha,\beta) \tag{3.2}$$
$$\Sigma_{Eq_2}(\alpha) = \Sigma_{Eq_2}(\beta) \leftrightarrow Eq_2(\alpha,\beta), \tag{3.3}$$

where Eq_1, Eq_2 are equivalence relations, and $\Sigma_{Eq_1}, \Sigma_{Eq_2}$ are the abstraction operators yielded by Eq_1, Eq_2 respectively, the identity statement

$$\Sigma_{Eq_1}(\alpha) = \Sigma_{Eq_2}(\beta) \tag{3.4}$$

cannot be decided by the related APs. For instance, consider the natural number 2 introduced by HP and the real number 2 introduced by e.g. RATIO – see Section 2.5. Neither HP nor RATIO establish whether the natural number 2 is identical with the real number 2.

criteria for singulartermhood, HP-terms are singular terms denoting objects. As Wright (2020, p. 306) puts it,

> [t]o solve the Caesar problem is not to show that terms introduced by good abstractions refer. But it is – or so I have suggested – to meet a necessary condition for showing that.

In Section 4.3, we'll see how Neologicists propose to solve CP by metaphysical principles. For the remainder of this section, let us focus on two other solutions to CP: *conventionalism* and *deflationism*.

The guiding idea of the former is that, like the truth of APs is putatively fixed by stipulation (see Section 5.3), further stipulations can determine the truth or falsehood of "mixed" identities. Conventionalism is a "piecemeal" approach (Studd 2023, p. 237): At any given moment, linguistic stipulation can determine some, but possibly not all, cross-sortal identities left open by APs. Versions of conventionalism are defended also by Rayo (2013, pp. 80–81) and Linnebo (2018, p. 160).

According to deflationism, as in, for example, Antonelli (2010a,b), the role of APs is to provide an "inflationary thrust" on the first-order domain by "giv[ing] a lower bound on the cardinality of the domain of objects, relative to the size of the class of all concepts, taken *modulo* a given equivalence relation."[91] According to Antonelli, APs do not provide information about the nature of these objects; by contrast, anything can be an abstract object, provided that it belongs to a domain with the appropriate cardinality. This proves to be a dissolution of CP, since, for example, $\#X$ is identical to Caesar in some models of HP and distinct from Caesar in other models.[92]

4 Philosophical Abstractionism II: Ontology

4.1 Introduction

Traditionally, APs are defended along with realist ontologies (in particular, Platonism). *Platonism* is typically characterized by two claims:[93] There exists a realm of abstract objects to which mathematical language refers and that is described by our mathematical theories; and these objects exist and have their

---

[91] Antonelli (2010a, p. 192).

[92] Antonelli (2010a,b); see also Boccuni and Woods (2020) and Section 2.7. Boccuni and Woods (2020) defend a similar view based on a reading of HP-terms as arbitrary names. Particularly, Boccuni and Woods's (2020) notion of *weak invariance* is used to capture the view that, for "$\Sigma\alpha$" to be genuinely referential, there is no need for "$\Sigma\alpha$" to refer to a particular object – with a peculiar nature. All that is required for (genuine) referentiality is that, e.g. "$\#X$" refers to *any* object of any domain satisfying HP.

[93] Linnebo (2018, p. 189).

properties independently of mathematicians and their thoughts, language, and practices. We will first show how abstractionists defend the existence claim (Sections 4.2–4.2.2). We will then consider various ways in which the independence claim can be cashed out (Section 4.2.3).[94] Finally, in Section 4.3, we consider the view that APs characterize the intrinsic nature of the objects that these principles introduce.

4.2 The Existence of Mathematical Objects

As seen in Section 3.2, the Neologicist defense of Platonism is based on three premisses.[95] The first premise concerns the logical form of the left-hand side of APs:

(1) The numerical terms that appear on the left of APs are singular terms.

Premise (1) is syntactic because abstractionists claim that it is possible to identify singular terms independently of any consideration of the semantic role of these expressions – see Section 3.2.

The second premise expresses a sufficient condition for singular terms to refer:

(2) A singular term t refers, and hence the object to which it refers exists, if t appears in a *true* (extensional) sentential context, and specifically in true identity statements.

Premise (2) should be uncontroversial: Given the standard semantic clauses for first-order logic, "$t = t'$" is satisfied by a structure $M = \langle D, I \rangle$ if, and only if, $I(t) = I(t')$.[96]

---

[94] The views discussed in this section are similar to the proposal in Zalta (1983). Zalta claims that mathematical theories, and arithmetic in particular, can be reduced to an axiomatic theory of abstract objects – which Zalta calls *object theory*. In object theory, abstract objects are introduced by a comprehension principle, which asserts that for any condition ϕ expressed in a modal higher-order language $\mathscr{L}_\diamond$ there is an object that "encodes" property X if, and only if, X satisfies ϕ. The instances of this principle explicitly assert the existence of abstract objects. Zalta claims that mathematical truths can be reduced to truths about abstract objects in this theory, and that this motivates a form of logicism (Linsky and Zalta 2006).

[95] This presentation is based on Hale and Wright (2009b); early expositions of the view relied more heavily on the Syntactic Priority Thesis (Section 3.2) as a motivation for the second premise.

[96] It is worth noting that, if the background logic is classical, any singular term is referential regardless of the present argument. However, Neologicists have independently suggested that their position should be cashed out using a *free logic* – see e.g. Hale and Wright (2009a, p. 463). In a *negative* free logic, in particular, any atomic predication involving a singular term t is deemed as false unless t is referential; therefore, "$t = t$" can be understood as asserting the existence of t – see Linnebo (2018, Appendix 2B, pp. 48–49); see also Payne (2013b, chapter 2), Tennant (2022), and Conti (2020).

Finally, the third premise asserts that there are true instances of the right-hand side of HP:

(3) There are true instances of the right-hand side of APs.

These instances include, for example, statements of the equinumerosity of a concept with itself.[97]

Since there are true instances of its right-hand side, and HP is a material biconditional, then there are also true instances of the left-hand side of HP. Combined with (1), it follows that there are true identity statements between singular terms. And since the left-hand side meets the condition specified in (2) for ensuring that a singular term refers to an object that exists, then numerical terms refer to objects, and so there are numbers.[98]

The *logical assumptions* of this argument consist in the second-order comprehension schema CA, which states that there is a concept X corresponding to any formula $\phi(x)$ (with x that occurs free in ϕ). For example, to show that 0 exists, Neologicists consider a concept whose extension is (necessarily) empty, say, the concept of being not self-identical. The argument also assumes classical logic.[99] The only nonlogical assumption of the argument is Hume's Principle. HP states that statements that feature numerical terms are materially equivalent to statements that do not feature these terms.[100]

The abstractionist ontology of mathematics faces, however, the following *problem of the origin*. Assume that APs can be stipulated without presupposing

---

[97] Note that it is a theorem of second-order logic that $X \approx X$ for any X. For an overview of second-order logic (SOL), see Section 2.2.

[98] Note that since (1) and (2) are background assumptions that do not concern mathematical objects in particular, the existence of these objects would follow from (3) alone, that is, from the true instances of the right-hand side. In the case of HP and other second-order APs, we can get these truths by higher-order logic alone.

[99] See footnote 96.

[100] Premise (2) corresponds to what Neologicists refer to as *minimalism* in meta-ontology. MacBride (2003) claims that Neologicism requires a "plastic" conception, reminiscent of Carnap and Putnam, according to which reality has its structure imposed on it by our language – see also MacBride (2016, pp. 95–96). Eklund (2006) and Hawley (2007) claim that Neologicists are, or should be, committed to *maximalism*, namely the view that everything that can possibly exist does actually exist. Finally, Sider (2007) claims that Neologicism should rely on *quantifier variance* as formulated by Eli Hirsch. Neologicists have denied that their view incurs in these further commitments – Hale and Wright (2009b). Finally, Hume's Principle features prominently in Amie Thomasson's *easy ontology* approach (see Thomasson 2013, 2014). According to Thomasson, ontological disputes can be settled by "trivial arguments [leading] us from uncontroversial premises to conclude that the relevant entities exist" (Thomasson 2013, p. 1023). Thomasson claims, in particular, that there are Ks if, and only if, the application conditions associated with the concept K are fulfilled (Thomasson 2014, p. 86). The existence of numbers can be derived from the uncontroversial premise that there are as many Xs as Ys modulo the conceptual truth that the number of X = the number of Y if, and only if, X and Y are equinumerous.

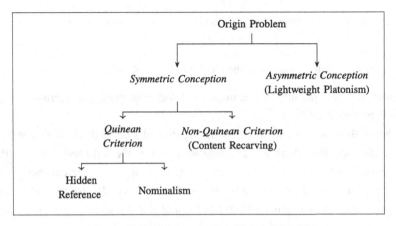

Figure 1 Responses to the origin problem.

the existence of mathematical objects. Let's also assume that pure higher-order logic is ontologically neutral, as Neologicists do (Wright 2007; Hale 2019), rather than "set theory in sheep's clothing" (Quine 1970, chapter 5). Abstractionists must explain how the ontological commitment of mathematical theories originates if both SOL and AP are not committed to the existence of objects of a particular sort. For example, if the right-hand side of HP is not committed to the existence of numbers, then its left-hand side is not committed to the existence of numbers either. Vice versa, if the left of HP does carry a commitment to numbers, then by contrapositive reasoning, the right-hand side carries the exact same commitment. But since some true instances of the right of HP are purely second-order logical truths, then SOL is not ontologically innocent.

The different responses to this problem are tabled in Figure 1. First, we can distinguish between *asymmetric* and *symmetric* conceptions of abstraction (see Linnebo 2018, §1.7). According to the symmetric conception, the two sides of APs have the same ontological commitments. Among these positions, we can distinguish between those that adopt the Quinean criterion according to which the ontological commitment of a theory consists in what must lie in the range of its (first-order) quantifiers in order for the statements of that theory to be true, and those that reject this criterion.[101] According to the asymmetric conceptions, by contrast, the commitments of the left of an AP exceeds those

---

[101] It is worth noting that an advocate of the symmetric view that the two sides have one and the same content must either reject the Quinean criterion or else conclude that this criterion fails to be invariant with respect to content *recarving* (see Section 4.2.2); we are grateful to an anonymous reviewer for this suggestion.

of its right.[102] We will consider these positions proceeding from the bottom to the top of Figure 1.

4.2.1 Quinean Criterion: Hidden Reference and Nominalism

It is natural to assume that the left-hand side of APs can commit to the existence of abstract objects only if the right-hand side carries the same commitment. For example, Wright claims that "the existence of numbers is [not] a *further* fact, something which the (mere) equinumerosity of concepts may leave unresolved" (Wright 1999, in Hale and Wright 2001a, p. 312, italic in the original). By adopting the Quinean criterion, either both sides are ontologically committed to mathematical objects or neither side is.[103]

The first view was briefly entertained by Neologicists under the label of "hidden reference." According to this view, the right-hand side of APs "achieves a reference to [abstract objects] without containing any particular part which so refers" (Wright 1983, p. 33; see also Hale and Wright 2001a, pp. 205–207).

Versions of mathematical nominalism, that is, the view that there are no abstract objects, were proposed by Florio and Leach-Krouse (2017), Schindler (2021), and Urbaniak (2010). According to these accounts, neither of the two sides of APs *refers* to abstract objects; on the contrary, the function of APs would be purely expressive. In particular, sentences that feature terms for abstract objects would allow us to convey, in a concise way, equivalent higher-order logical contents.[104] Let's give an example. Schindler presents a position, akin to alethic deflationism, according to which the concept *Number* is exhausted by the *Numerical Equivalence Schema*:

(NES) $\#X = n \leftrightarrow \exists_n x(Xx)$,

where $\exists_n x(Xx)$ abbreviates "there are nX's."[105] The right of NES features the "numerically definite quantifiers" "$\exists_0$," "$\exists_1$," and so on, whereas its left features singular numerical terms "0" and "1." First-order quantification over n is possible on the left but not on the right; therefore, the purpose of number

---

[102] The asymmetric conception usually relies on the Quinean criterion; see Linnebo (2018, pp. 13–14).

[103] HP is indeed first-orderly *impredicative*, i.e. the domain of the first-order quantifiers on its right include cardinal numbers; cf. Section 2.6.

[104] It is worth noting since numerical terms do not refer to anything, "mixed" identity statements such as "The number of X = Julius Caesar" are deemed false (Urbaniak 2010, p. 167); see Section 3.4.

[105] The meaning of $\exists_n x(Xx)$ is defined recursively as: $\exists_0 x(Xx)$ if, and only if, $\neg \exists x(Xx)$; $\exists_1 x(Xx)$ if, and only if, $\exists x(Xx \wedge \forall y(Xy \rightarrow x = y)))$; and $\exists_{n+1} xX(x)$ if, and only if, $\exists x(Xx \wedge \exists_n y(Xy \wedge x \neq y))$.

talk is "to quantify (indirectly) into a position that our ordinary quantifiers are incapable of" (p. 868; for a similar view, see Hodes in Section 3.3.2).

4.2.2 Content Recarving

The *non-Quinean* criterion of ontological commitment is based on the idea that the two sides of APs share the same content.

A version of this idea was introduced by Frege himself, who in §64 of *Grundlagen* (p. 71) claimed that the concept *Direction* can be introduced by taking the right-hand side of the corresponding AP "as an identity":

> The judgment "line *a* is parallel to line *b*", or, using symbols, "*a//b*", can be taken as an identity. If we do this, we obtain the concept of direction, and say: "the direction of line *a* is identical with the direction of line *b*". Thus we replace the symbol // by the more generic symbol =, through removing what is specific in the content of the former and dividing it between *a* and *b*. We carve up the content in a way different from the original way, and this yields us a new concept.[106]

Frege's metaphor was followed, most notably, by Hale and Wright, who claim that the left-hand side of an instance of HP corresponds to a "reconceptualization" of its right-hand side (Wright 1999, p. 312). This proposal has been criticized by Fine (2002) and by Potter and Smiley (2001, 2002).[107] More recently, Fregean semantics has been defended by Rayo (2013).[108]

Rayo calls his position *trivialism*. Specifically, *Trivialist Platonism* (about finite cardinals) is the view that all the instances of the following schema are (trivially)[109] true:

NUMBERS: For the number of the X's to be *n just is* for there to be *n X*'s.

HP entails that for any finite n, $\#(X) = n \leftrightarrow \exists_n x(X(X))$. Under plausible assumptions about the logic of the "just is"-operator, NUMBERS follows from this version of HP (where $\equiv$ is the "just is"-operator):

$$\#X = \#Y \equiv X \approx Y.$$

---

[106] Frege (1884, §64).

[107] At the heart of this criticisms is the idea that any account of propositional equivalence under *recarving* that satisfies that the left-hand side of an instance of an AP is a recarving of its right-hand side is also trivial, i.e. entails that any pairs of sentences are one a "recarving" of the other; cf. Fine (2002, pp. 39–41).

[108] See Linnebo (2018, chapter 4, §4.3) for some objections to Rayo's account.

[109] A statement has trivial truth-conditions if, and only if, it has the same truth-conditions of logical plenitudes; see Section 4.2.3.

Rayo claims that "just is"-statements such as Numbers are "no difference" statements: For example, there is *no difference* between the number of the dinosaurs being zero and there being no dinosaurs (Rayo 2013, p. 4).

The nondifference claim is understood in terms of *sameness of facts*: Rayo claims that the two sides of NUMBERS provide "[a] full and accurate description of the same feature of reality" (Rayo 2013, p. 6). Rayo regiments his claim in terms of (sameness of) *truth-conditions*. This notion is explicated, in turn, in terms of (the identical) *demands* that the truth of two sentences make on the world (Rayo 2013, p. 52). Finally, Rayo claims that the sentence ϕ has the same ontological commitment as ψ if $\phi \equiv \psi$. This notion of ontological commitment differs from the Quinean one in that sentences with different logical forms can nonetheless make the same demands on the world (Rayo 2007).

Let's give an example. Suppose that we do accept that the two sides of the direction principle have the same ontological commitment (in Rayo's sense). Now consider a particular line a. Since we accept this "just is"-statement, we accept also that for the direction of a to be self-identical, and hence for that direction to exist, just is for a to be parallel to itself. Therefore, the direction of a exists, and so there are directions; however, the existence of directions does not require more from the world than what is required for two lines to be parallel.[110]

4.2.3 Lightweight Platonism

Linnebo (2018) recently put forward a version of the asymmetric conception. Linnebo claims that abstract objects are *thin* "in the sense that very little is required for their existence" (p. 3). More specifically, the truth of the right-hand side of an AP would be *sufficient* (in a technical sense) for the truth of its left-hand side. He calls this view *minimalism*.[111]

To set the stage, let's consider an example. The assertibility conditions for statements that involve direction-terms can plausibly be given by stating that "$x_1 = x_2$" is assertible of lines a_1 and a_2 if, and only if, $a_1 // a_2$, and "$P(Dir(a_1), \ldots, Dir(a_n))$" is assertible of $a_1, \ldots, a_n$ if, and only if, $a_P(a_1, \ldots, a_n)$, where x_1, x_n are variables for lines, P stands for an n-ary relation

---

[110] This is not the only way in which trivialism can be developed; according to Rayo, Numbers is just one possible example of "just-is"-statement that we could accept, but one could also accept that the axioms of Peano Arithmetic have trivial truth-conditions, i.e., PA $\equiv T$ with T being a logical truth (see Rayo 2013, pp. 179–191).

[111] Minimalism corresponds to an *asymmetric* conception of abstraction: The ontological commitments of the left of APs exceed those of their right; however, the obtaining of equivalence relations among nonmathematical entities is sufficient for mathematical objects to exist.

among directions, and α_P is an n-ary relation that is a congruence with respect to parallelism.

In first approximation, Linnebo defines sufficiency as follows: ϕ suffices for ψ if, and only if, ϕ is a ground for asserting ψ.[112] Given the assertibility aforementioned conditions, the AP for direction corresponds to the following sufficiency claims:

- $a_1//a_2 \Rightarrow Dir(a_1) = Dir(a_2)$
- $\neg a_1//a_2 \Rightarrow \neg Dir(a_1) = Dir(a_2)$

Suppose that lines a_1 and a_2 are parallel. $a//b$ is a sufficient ground to assert that $Dir(a_1) = Dir(a_2)$. Given the *nonreductive interpretation* of the extended language that Linnebo favors, direction-terms actually refer to directions.

Linnebo claims APs satisfy the following *Ontological Expansiveness Constraint*: There are sufficiency statements $\phi \Rightarrow \psi$ such that the ontological commitments of ψ exceed those of ϕ (Linnebo 2018: pp. 13–17). In particular, the left-hand side of an AP can carry more commitment than its right-hand side, even if the truth of the latter is sufficient for the truth of the former. Linnebo's view amounts, therefore, to an asymmetric conception of abstraction. At the same time, Linnebo emphasizes that his view yields a form of *lightweight* Platonism, according to which mathematical objects, unlike ordinary ones, require little from the world in order to exist.[113]

Linnebo suggests that his notion of sufficiency can be explicated by the notion of metaphysical explanation or *grounding* (Clark and Liggins 2012; Fine 2012).[114] Linnebo claims that "the sufficiency statements can be seen as recording grounding potentials" (Linnebo 2018, p. 43, footnote 41). Linnebo's talk of "grounding potentials" can be clarified as follows. Suppose that the right-hand side of an AP indeed suffices for the truth of its left-hand side. Then, if it is the case that the right-hand side is true, then the right-hand side grounds the left-hand side. This view has been proposed by Rosen (2010) and Schwartzkopff (2011) and developed by Donaldson (2017). It yields a version of lightweight Platonism.[115]

---

[112] Linnebo's technical definition is more complex; see Linnebo (2018, p. 140).

[113] As Linnebo (2023a) himself points out, the "independence claim" of Platonism (see Section 4.1) is intended to convey an analogy between mathematical and physical objects; *lightweight Platonism* is any view that accepts both the existence and mind-independence of mathematical objects, but weakens the analogy with ordinary objects.

[114] Even though he claims the notion cannot be identified with *grounding*; see Linnebo (2018, p. 18).

[115] Note that the symmetric conception of abstraction is incompatible with ground-theoretic APs assuming that grounding is irreflexive.

To formulate APs as claims of grounding, let's introduce the sentential operator $<$ for full,[116] immediate,[117] and strict[118] ground.[119] A natural proposal to state a "metaphysical" version of an AP is claiming that $\alpha \sim \beta$ fully, immediately, and strictly grounds $\Sigma\alpha = \Sigma\beta$. However, grounding is a *factive* notion: If A (metaphysically) explains B, then both A and B are the case. The principle would therefore entail that $\alpha \sim \beta$ for any α and β. Moreover, since the principle entails that $\Sigma\alpha = \Sigma\beta$, this principle would also "prejudge" the existence of abstract objects (Schwartzkopff 2011, p. 362, footnote 18).

Both problems can be solved by adopting conditionalized versions of ground-theoretic APs similar to Linnebo's. These principles provide an account of what grounds identities between abstract objects. However, it is silent about *inequalities*, that is, each case in which the two items have different abstracts. At the same time, an AP states that $\alpha \sim \beta$ is sufficient *and necessary* for $\Sigma\alpha$ and $\Sigma\beta$ to be identical. Therefore, it is natural to extend the principle by adding that not only if $\Sigma\alpha = \Sigma\beta$, then $\alpha \sim \beta$ grounds $\Sigma\alpha = \Sigma\beta$, but also if $\Sigma\alpha \neq \Sigma\beta$, then $\neg(\alpha \sim \beta)$ grounds $\Sigma\alpha \neq \Sigma\beta$ – see Donaldson (2017, pp. 785–786), Linnebo (2023b), and deRosset and Linnebo (2023).

For example, suppose that there are as many cities in Wales as species of Flamingo.[120] It is natural to think that the fact that the numbers of the cities of Wales and the species of Flamingo are identical is grounded by the fact that these cities and these species can be paired one-to-one, but this latter fact is not grounded by the fact that their number is the same.

According to its proponents, the ground-theoretic formulation of HP, or variants thereof, vindicates a form of *Aristotelianism* in the philosophy of mathematics (Rosen 2011, 2016; Donaldson 2017, p. 776). Aristotle claimed that mathematical objects are not separate substances, but rather exist "in" physical entities, and are reached by abstraction of some of the characteristic properties of these entities. According to Aristotelianism, mathematical objects are therefore dependent entities (Schwartzkopff 2011). Unlike in Aristotle's view, however, these objects do not exist "in" physical ones, but their existence is grounded in empirical facts (Horsten and Leitgeb 2009).

---

[116] A set of sentences Γ fully grounds A if the former provides a completely satisfactory metaphysical explanation of the latter, while Γ *partially* grounds A if the former helps to ground the latter.

[117] Γ immediately grounds A if, and only if, there is no fact "in between" the ground and the grounded; Γ *mediately* grounds A otherwise.

[118] Γ strictly grounds A if for any set of facts Δ that contains A, there is no fact $B \in \Gamma$ that is mediately grounded by Δ.

[119] Alternatively, grounding can be construed as a relation among facts; see Correia and Schnieder (2012).

[120] This exotic example is due to Donaldson (2017, p. 792).

4.3 Real Definitions

Another claim that characterizes some abstractionist positions is that APs provide *real definitions*, that is, definitions of the essence of the objects introduced by these principles.

Real definitions have the form, "What is for something to be an X is to be a Y." We will adopt Fine's notation "$\Box_x A$" to assert that a truth A belongs to the essence of x (Fine 1995a).[121] We can now distinguish between three different claims, even though these are often intertwined with each other (cf. Hale 2013, 2019).

The first, and relatively uncontroversial, claim is that if an AP is consistent, then the function Σ is essentially governed by AP:

(I) $\Box_\Sigma \, \forall \alpha \forall \beta \, (\Sigma\alpha = \Sigma\beta \leftrightarrow \alpha \sim \beta)$

The second claim, which is also relatively uncontroversial,[122] is that to be a Σ-abstract, which we denote by "$@_\Sigma(x)$," is for something to be the value of Σ for some α:

(II) $\Box_{@_\Sigma} \, @_\Sigma(x) \leftrightarrow \exists \alpha \, (x = \Sigma\alpha)$

Finally, the third and more controversial claim is that Σ-abstracts are essentially the values of Σ – that is, if x is a Σ-abstract, then being a Σ-abstract is part of x's essence:

(III) $@_\Sigma(x) \rightarrow \Box_x \, @_\Sigma(x)$

This final claim entails that abstraction functions are *generative* in Rosen and Yablo's (2020) sense, that is, its values are essentially values of that function. As noted by Rosen and Yablo, claiming that the cardinality function is generative is sufficient to settle "mixed" identities and therefore to provide a solution to the Caesar problem (Section 3.4): Since it does not belong to the nature of Julius Caesar to be the number of some concept, then Caesar cannot be a number.

The Caesar Problem could indeed be solved by adding application conditions to HP. Neologicists claim, however, that such an extension is not necessary (Wright 1983, p. 116; Hale and Wright 2001b). They argue that such conditions

---

[121] Fine (1995b) distinguishes between *constitutive essence*, to indicate those truths that directly defines essence, and *consequential essence*, to indicate the closure of constitutive essence under logical consequence; the relevant notion here is that of consequential essence.

[122] The reason why (I) are (II) seem uncontroversial is that the abstraction function Σ and the predicate $abstr_\Sigma(x)$ are purportedly defined, implicitly or explicitly, by AP and by $@_\Sigma(x) \leftrightarrow \exists \alpha \, (x = \Sigma\alpha)$, respectively.

can be derived indirectly from the identity conditions that HP does provide.[123] To this aim, Neologicists rely on the principle N^d:

N^d: Y is a sortal concept under which numbers fall (if? and) only if there could be singular terms "a" and "b" denoting instances of Y such that the truth-conditions of "$a = b$" are the same as those of some statement of equinumerosity between a pair of concepts.[124]

In general, provided that the truth-conditions of identity criteria for persons are not given in terms of one-to-one correspondence, from N^d it follows that no cardinals are persons. N^d follows, in its turn, from HP together with a yet more general *Principle of Sortal Inclusion* (SIP) that Neologicists deem as independently plausible:[125]

SIP: A sort of objects X is included within a sort Y only if the content of a suitable range of identity statements about Ys – those linking terms denoting Ys that are candidates to be Xs – is the same as that of statements asserting satisfaction of the criterion of identity for the corresponding Xs.[126]

SIP entails that Caesar is not a cardinal number if he is a person. This line of reasoning can be generalized to any sortal concept under which objects that are not cardinals fall.[127]

Hale's and Wright's solution to CP yields a form of mathematical Platonism according to which mathematical objects are conceived as *sui generis* entities. However, Hale (2018) highlights a possible tension between essentialism and the Neologicist epistemology of mathematics, according to which the truth of APs can be stipulated (cf. Section 5.3.1), whereas it plausibly cannot be stipulated that some objects have a certain essence.[128]

---

[123] See e.g. Wright (1983, p. 114).

[124] Wright (1983, pp. 116–117).

[125] A *sortal* concept is provided both with an *identity criterion*, which states necessary and sufficient conditions for two objects that fall under that concept to be identical, and an *application criterion*, which states necessary and sufficient conditions for an object to fall under it. Neologicists restrict their attention to *pure* sortals that characterize the *nature* of the objects that fall under it (Hale 2001a, p. 387).

[126] Hale and Wright (2001a, p. 198); see also Hale and Wright (2001b, p. 370) and Wright (1983, p. 122).

[127] Since different sortals may share their identity conditions, but differ with respect to applications, Neologicists investigate *categories*, i.e. *maximally extensive sortals*, namely sortals all of whose sub-sortals share the same identity conditions, and such that any object to which that category does not apply must not fall under sortals not associated with those identity conditions (Hale and Wright 2001b).

[128] Hale attempts to ease this tension by arguing that cardinal numbers are "artificial kinds" whose essence is fixed by stipulation and can, therefore, be known a priori (Hale 2019, p. 2012).

Finally, the claim that cardinal numbers are *sui generis* objects distinguishes the brands of abstractionism that endorse it from other positions in the philosophy of mathematics. For example, Neologicists claim that the natural numbers are fundamentally cardinal numbers, whereas *structuralists* claim that natural numbers are essentially ordinals (Assadian and Buijsman 2018). We will return to the interplay between abstractionism and structuralism in Section 6.

5 Philosophical Abstractionism III: Epistemology

5.1 Introduction

This section surveys the main epistemological theses in the literature on abstractionism. We consider two epistemic puzzles[129]: How epistemic access to abstract objects can be attained through abstraction over equivalence relations (Section 5.2), and how APs themselves can be known, or at least blamelessly believed, as a result of their stipulation. This second challenge figures prominently in the Neologicist project. As we will see, the Neologicist epistemology of mathematics is centered around three notions: *arrogance*, *presupposition*, and *entitlement* (Section 5.3). We will finally consider some objections (Section 5.4).

5.2 Puzzle 1: Epistemic Access

The *access problem* is a traditional objection to Platonism (Panza and Sereni 2013, pp. 1–9). Platonism is the view that mathematical theories describe a realm of self-standing objects that exist and have their properties independently of mathematicians and their thoughts, language, and practices. However, Platonists must explain how mathematical knowledge is possible if these objects are abstract entities, not located in space and time and causally isolated from us (Linnebo 2009b, §4.2). A contemporary formulation of the problem is due to Benacerraf (1973). Benacerraf claims that a satisfactory account of mathematical truth must satisfy two conditions: a *semantic constraint* that requires that the semantic clauses for mathematical statements must be similar to the clauses for nonmathematical ones,[130] and an *epistemological constraint* that requires that this account must be compatible with the possibility of having

---

[129] We are grateful to an anonymous reviewer for the suggestion.

[130] In Benacerraf's words, "any theory of mathematical truth [should] be in conformity with a general theory of truth" (p. 408). Benacerraf considers the sentences "There are at least three large cities older than New York" and "There are at least three perfect numbers greater than 17." He argues that the explanation of the truth of these sentences must be similar, namely that there are at least three objects that have all a given property.

mathematical knowledge. Benacerraf claims that mathematical Platonism cannot satisfy both these criteria (pp. 674–675; see Hale and Wright (2002) for an assessment of Benacerraf's challenge). Assuming Platonism (see Section 4), this puzzle applies to abstractionism in mathematics in general.

Specifically in the case of finite cardinals, Neologicists claim that Frege's question – "How, then, are numbers given to us, if we cannot have any ideas or intuitions of them?" (Frege 1884, §62) – can be answered by an appeal to Hume's Principle. To illustrate their point, consider again Frege's example concerning directions, that is, direction of line a equals direction of line b if, and only if, a and b are parallel. Imagine three segments a, b, and c, such that a are b and parallel, and b is orthogonal to c. These latter facts can be ascertained by looking at the lines only. However, the AP for direction implies that two lines have the same direction if they are parallel. Therefore, if the AP for directions is interpreted in the way suggested by Neologicists, it seems possible to acquire inferential justification for our beliefs that concern abstract objects on the basis of our perceptual acquaintance with particular concrete objects.[131]

The Neologicist epistemology of mathematical objects rests on two considerations. (i) First, at least for some X and Y, knowing that X and Y can be paired one-to-one does not require knowing that their number is identical – or, indeed, that any number exists (Hale and Wright 2001a, p. 10). For example, Wright (1998) calls two concepts X and Y *unproblematic* if knowledge of whether they are instantiated by some numbers is not needed to determine whether these concepts can be put into one-to-one correspondence.[132] An example of unproblematic concept is *Conqueror of Gaul*. An example of a problematic concept is, by contrast, *identical to either one or two*. Nonproblematic concepts ensure that epistemic justification can be transmitted from the right to the left of an AP. (ii) The epistemology of Hume's Principle must be similarly unproblematic, as is clarified in Section 5.3.

As regards abstractionism in general, a version of the epistemic access problem was formulated in Field (1989). According to Field, the challenge is to explain how (the justification for) our mathematical beliefs can be *reliable*, that is, how it is responsive to the truth of those beliefs if we can have no access to the mathematical domain (p. 26). This epistemological challenge targets the view that the mathematical domain is *insulated* from the physical domain (Rosen 1993, pp. 151–153). In Field's words, "our belief in a theory should be

---

[131] See Rosen (1993, pp. 155–158). However, this account will not generalize as most APs, e.g. HP, do not appeal to concrete objects on their right.

[132] Plebani, San Mauro, and Venturi (2023) introduce a notion of *transparency* that nicely captures this requirement.

undermined if the theory requires that it would be a huge coincidence if what we believed about its subject matter were correct" (Field 2005, p. 77). However, abstractionism has the means to answer this challenge, as explained in what follows.

Linnebo (2018) offers the following account of how APs determine the truth of mathematical statements, and, at the same time, they explain the reliability of mathematicians' beliefs (pp. 201–204). First, he shows that APs meet an epistemic constraint. This constraint requires that, if ϕ suffices for ψ, then it must be possible to know the corresponding conditional $\phi \rightarrow \psi$ (p. 16). In Linnebo's account (see Sections 2.6 and 4.2.3 in this volume), these conditionals correspond to *language extensions*, such that the left-hand side of APs is assertible if the right-hand side is. If such language extension is carried out, one obtains the relevant conditional "for free" (p. 202).[133] According to Linnebo, the truth of the right-hand side is then sufficient (in a technical sense) for the truth of the left-hand side, and so for abstract objects to exists. As he points out, "the less of a demand the existence of mathematical objects makes on the world, the easier it will be to know that the demand is satisfied" (p. 10).

The model proposed by Rayo (2013) is as follows. Suppose that an AP is stipulated as a contextual definition of the cardinality operator. In this case, a justification for (an instance of) the right-hand side of this AP will itself count as a justification for (the corresponding instance of) its left-hand side, since these sides are, by stipulation, materially equivalent (p. 98). More generally, Rayo claims that mathematical statements have trivial truth-conditions, that is, that nothing in the world is required for these statements to be true (Section 4.2.2). As he points out, "this means, in particular, that there is no need to go to the world to check whether any requirements have been met in order to determine whether the truth-conditions of a truth of pure mathematics are satisfied" (p. 98).

5.3 Puzzle 2: Knowledge by Abstraction

The most distinctive claim of the abstractionist tradition is that APs allow claiming the *aprioricity* of the mathematical theories that can be derived from them:[134] "The abstractionist program of foundations for classical mathematical theories is, like its traditional logicist ancestors, first and foremost an *epistemological* project. Its official aim is to demonstrate the possibility of a certain

---

[133] Suppose for example that $a // b$, i.e. a is parallel to b; then $Dir(a) = Dir(b)$; by conditional proof, $a // b \rightarrow Dir(a) = Dir(b)$.

[134] See e.g. Hale and Wright (2000) and Wright (2016).

uniform mode of *a priori* knowledge of the basic laws of arithmetic, real and complex analysis, and set theory" (Wright 2016, p. 161).

In the case of arithmetic, the defense of this view rests on three claims:

(i) HP can be known a priori, or at least blamelessly believed, as a result of its stipulation as an implicit definition.

(ii) (i) guarantees that the translations of the axioms of PA^2 in the language of FA – call these translations $PA^{2^\#}$ – can be known a priori.

(iii) The concept of cardinal number introduced by HP is the (ordinary) concept of *cardinal number*; moreover, the concepts of 0, successor and natural numbers defined in terms of $\#$ are the ordinary arithmetical concepts.

If (i) and (ii) hold, then $PA^{2^\#}$ are a priori. But, given (iii), $PA^{2^\#}$ are the axioms of PA^2 – rather than a set of sentences with the same form. Therefore, PA^2 is a priori (e.g. Hale and Wright 2001a, pp. 11–13).[135]

Let's consider (i), (ii), and (iii) in their turn.

5.3.1 Arrogance, Presuppositions, and Entitlement

One of the central claims of Neologicism is that Hume's Principle and other abstractions are a priori. Traditionally, Neologicists mean what Field (2005) calls *strong aprioricity* or *empirical indefeasibility*: Hume's Principle is a priori in the sense that it admits no empirical evidence against it.[136] The Neologicist epistemology of abstraction rests on a triad: *arrogance, presupposition,* and *entitlement.*

The argument for the *aprioricity* of Hume's Principle rests on what Wright and Hale calls the "traditional connection" between analyticity and *aprioricity*: "if the stipulation has the effect that ['$\#$'] and hence [HP] are fully understood – ...then nothing will stand in the way of an intelligent disquotation: the knowledge that '[HP] is true' will extend to knowledge that [HP]" (Hale and Wright 2000, pp. 126–127, modified). This connection requires not only that HP does provide a successful implicit definition (hence, the Neologicist semantic claim) but also that HP is – in their terms – *nonarrogant,* that is, its truth can be

---

135 Abstractionists would plausibly claim that PA^2 is a priori even if some arithmetical truths, for example Gödel's sentence, cannot be known on the basis of HP; see e.g. Pregel (2023).

136 A proposition is *weakly* a priori, by contrast, if it can be rationally believed without empirical evidence. Hume's Principle is *conservative,* that is, it has no consequence for the "old" ontology of any theory T to which it can be consistently added that are not already consequences of T alone (see Section 2.8). Let T be any theory that has observable consequences and to which HP can be consistently added. Given the conservativeness of HP, any defeater of a prediction made by T extended with HP is already a defeater of T alone; this eliminates the possibility that HP can be, even in principle, empirically defeated (Hale and Wright 2000, p. 147).

stipulated without "collateral (a posteriori) epistemic work" (Hale and Wright 2000, p. 128).

Wright later distinguishes between two genres of presuppositions (Wright 2004a, pp. 189–191; Wright 2004b, p. 161; Wright 2020, pp. 292–294).[137] Presuppositions of the first type can obstruct the "traditional connection" between analyticity and *aprioricity*. The chief example given by Neologicists is the stipulation that Jack the Ripper is responsible for the London killings of 1888 as a means to bestow meaning on the name "Jack the Ripper" (Hale and Wright 2000, pp. 121–123). This statement is plausibly analytic (in the definitional sense); however, a subject could not achieve a priori knowledge that a single individual was responsible for those killings simply by inferring it from the stipulation, as this stipulation is "hostage" of the truth of the presupposition that the killings had a single perpetrator (Hale and Wright 2000, p. 121).[138]

Neologicists claim that Hume's Principle can be stipulated *without* presupposing that there are numbers (e.g. Wright 1999, pp. 309–312). They argue that, even though the truth of the left of HP requires that there are numbers, HP is a *biconditional* that states necessary and sufficient conditions for cardinal numbers to be identical. HP entails that there are numbers only "by appropriate input into (instances of) its right-hand side" (Wright 1999, p. 309), that is, in conjunction with the additional premise that X and Y are equinumerous. However, this premise is not made true by the stipulation of HP but is available independently from second-order logic. HP, by contrast, can be considered as a purely stipulative truth, and "the existence of numbers, and indeed their satisfaction of the Peano axioms, [is] a congenial discovery" (Wright 1990, p. 163) rather than a presupposition.[139]

The second kind of presuppositions are *inevitable* and, for this reason, compatible with a *default* epistemic warrant. Wright labels these propositions

---

[137] See Assadian (2023) for an analysis using Strawson's notion of presupposition.

[138] According to Neologicists, a stipulation that rests on substantial presupposition can still ground a priori knowledge provided that (i) the presupposition is something that "we can prove *independently*" (Wright 1998, p. 301, italic in the original), and (ii) this proof does not require a posteriori truths. For example, Boolos's New V presupposes that there are concepts that are "too big," i.e. with the same cardinality as the universe (see Section 2.6). However, as Wright notices, this presupposition is available independently "as a theorem of second-order logic" (Wright 1998, p. 301.).

[139] Neologicists imagine a subject, Hero, is competent in higher-order logic. They argue that Hero can grasp the concept of number on the basis of HP, and hence the meaning of each sentential context in which those terms occur and whose extra higher-order logical vocabulary that Hero already understands (Wright 1998, pp. 354–355). A specific worry concerns the *first-order impredicativity* of Hume's principle (cf. Section 2.6). Wright (1998) replies, however, that "it is not and *cannot* in general be a prerequisite for a quantified statement to be determinate – or determinate enough – in content that the range of its quantifiers should have been specified in advance" (p. 242, italic in the original).

cornerstones. He claims that any kind of cognitive project involves some pre-suppositions of this kind. In this case, there is "a rational ground to accept a proposition that consists neither in the possession of evidence for its truth, nor in the occurrence of any kind of cognitive achievement that would normally be regarded as apt to constitute knowledge of it" (Wright 2014, p. 213). Wright calls this kind of epistemic warrant absent defeaters *entitlement*. In Wright's view, a proposition p is an epistemic entitlement (EE) if the following three conditions are satisfied:

(i) p is *a presupposition with respect to a cognitive project*, i.e. to doubt p (in advance) would rationally commit one to doubt of the significance or competence of the project;

(ii) S has no sufficient reasons to believe that p is untrue;

(iii) the attempt to justify p would involve further presuppositions in turn of no more secure prior standing, and so without limit.

According to Wright, EES that satisfy these conditions are both *relative* to a cognitive project and *defeasible*. Wright distinguishes between different cases of entitlements of cognitive projects, in particular, entitlement to the epistemic cooperativeness of the environment and entitlement to trust one's cognitive faculties (Wright 2004a, 2004b). He also claims that "we are in general entitled to take it that the concepts in terms of which we formulate a project and its findings are in *good standing*" (Wright 2016, p. 168, italic in the original). Wright finally argues that an *entitlement to Hume's Principle* falls in this last category.

Specifically, condition (i) of Wright's EE is connected to the idea that entitlements are "authenticity conditions," that is, that anyone doubting them cannot rationally embark on the relevant project (Wright 2020, p. 292). HP can be seen as an arithmetical presupposition as long as doubting HP leads, via Frege's Theorem, to questioning the axioms of PA^2 (Pedersen 2016, p. 191). Moreover, HP is equi-consistent with PA^2, so there are no good reasons to think that HP is not consistent. Besides, proving the consistency of HP would require a theory at least as strong as PA^2 itself. So it cannot be required that a subject is already in a position to prove that HP is "in good standing" because they can trust its stipulation – see Section 5.4. HP seems therefore to satisfy conditions (ii) and (iii) as well.

Wright (2016) recants his former views and claims that Hume's Principle is a case of EE. The main difference between Wright's view and the Neologicist position is that HP is no longer deemed as known a priori (2016, p. 163).[140]

---

[140] Even if EE is still a case of a priori warrant; see (Wright 2020, p. 292).

He suggests, by contrast, that "the epistemology of good abstraction principles should be assimilated to that of basic principles of logical inference" (2016, p. 180) such as *modus ponens* (*MPP*). By that, Wright means that (i) the justification for both logical principles and APs is "beneath knowledge," if knowledge requires a form of inferential justification,[141] and that (ii) we have nonetheless a rational entitlement to take both logical principles and APs to be valid or true (Wright 2004a; Wright 2004b, pp. 167–169; Wright 2016, pp. 169–171). However, Wright argues that an entitlement to HP is sufficient to warrant a priori knowledge of the axioms of PA^2, as we will now see.

5.3.2 FA is A Priori

As regards (iii) – HP guarantees that the truths of Frege Arithmetic are a priori – this claim immediately follows if (a) HP is justified a priori and (b) a priori justification is closed under (known) second-order entailment. Neologicists claim that all the (second-order) logical consequences of HP are a priori. Frege's Theorem then shows that $PA^{2^\#}$ is a priori.[142]

Wright (2016) claims, moreover, that an EE to HP is sufficient to claim knowledge of its logical consequences and in particular of the Peano axioms (p. 179). To do this, Wright argues that HP can be compared to basic logical laws such as *MPP*. As seen, Wright thinks that *MPP* is an EE, that is, that there is an epistemic warrant, falling short of a priori justification, to trust the validity of this rule. According to Wright, this is compatible with the view that we can achieve inferential justification by deploying *MPP*. Suppose, for example, that a subject knows that ϕ and that $\phi \rightarrow \psi$. Wright argues that the subject can be credited with *knowledge* of ψ even though the subject is only entitled to *MPP*. The guiding thought is that since it is not possible to achieve full-fledged justification for *MPP*, it would be unreasonable to ask that a subject is justified in believing that *MPP* is valid before that subject can achieve justification by the means of *MPP* itself (Wright 2004b, pp. 166–169). To make the analogy between *MPP* and HP precise, Wright notices that the latter can be construed as a pair of introduction and elimination rules for the cardinality operator. Wright concludes that the consequences of HP, and the axioms of PA^2 proved in FA, can be known a priori even if the subject has only an entitlement to HP (Wright 2016, p. 175 ff.).

Let's see an example. Consider the translation in FA of the claim that zero is a natural number. "ℕ" is defined in FA as being either identical to 0 or standing

---

[141] Basic logical principles satisfies conditions (i)–(iii); see Wright (2004b).

[142] Neologicists claim, more precisely, that SOL transmits a priori justification, Wright has recently changed his view and no longer claims that HP is a priori, as mentioned in Section 5.3.1.

in the (weak) ancestral of the predecessor with 0 (see Section 2.4). Therefore, a subject can arguably claim knowledge of $\mathbb{N}(0)^{\#}$ if this subject can claim knowledge of $0 = 0$. This identity can be inferred by applying the right-to-left direction of HP to $x \neq x \approx x \neq x$. This last formula is a consequence of SOL. According to Wright, there is an entitlement to both the rules of SOL and to the pair of introduction and elimination rules for the cardinality operator $\#$ corresponding to the right-to-left and to the left-to-right directions of HP respectively, and no further premise is needed to derive the FA-translation of $0 = 0$. One also needs to assume the unrestricted comprehension schema CA. This use of CA has been criticized by Shapiro and Weir (2000). They formulate an "Aristotelian logic" in which comprehension is not allowed if the concept is empty. Neologicists defend CA on the basis of an *abundant conception of properties*, according to which there exists a property for any well-defined predicate (Hale 2019). It is unclear if Neologicists can claim EE also to that conception.[143] If so, then no other premises are needed, and, crucially, no other premise must be known a priori, to claim a priori knowledge that zero is a natural number.

5.3.3 Hermeneutic and Reconstructive Abstractionism

Let's turn to the third and final claim – the definitions in FA track "ordinary" arithmetical concepts. We can distinguish between *hermeneutic* and *reconstructive* (or modal) interpretations of abstractionism (MacBride 2003, pp. 130–132). As a hermeneutical project, by contrast, the aim of Neologicism is to show that HP grounds our actual mathematical thinking, that is, that Hume's Principle is "what we had in mind all along when we reasoned arithmetically" (MacBride 2003, p. 157). As a reconstructive project, the aim of abstractionism is to provide a rational reconstruction of arithmetical knowledge, that is, to show how this knowledge could in principle be attained on the basis of HP, regardless of whether this reconstruction mirrors the way in which mathematical truths are actually apprehended by ordinary thinkers.

Richard Kimberly Heck (Heck 1997b; see Postscript, in Heck 2011a, pp. 631–643) formulates an objection against hermeneutic abstractionism. Heck argues that (1) in order for abstractionism to succeed, "it must be possible to recognize the truth of HP by reflecting on fundamental features of arithmetical reasoning" (Heck 2011a, p. 589): HP, including the criterion for assigning cardinalities to infinite concepts that it embodies, must be implicit in ordinary arithmetical reasoning. However, (2) the possibility of a different assignment of

---

[143] For example, Moretti and Wright (2023) mention a kind of entitlement to "metaphysically heavyweight" propositions.

cardinal numbers to infinite concepts would show that "it is conceptually possible that HP is false" (Heck 2011a, p. 641), namely, it is possible that another principle, instead of HP, underlies our actual concept of *cardinal number*. Heck mentions theories of non-Cantorian cardinalities that preserve part–whole intuitions in support of their argument.

A recent version of Heck's objection is proposed by Mancosu (2016, chapter 3). Mancosu notices that there are infinitely many principles of the same form as HP that differ from this latter on the assignment of cardinal numbers to infinite concepts. An example is what Mancosu calls Peano's Principle (PP). This principle assigns one and the same cardinal number to every infinite concept and cardinal numbers to finite concepts in the same way as HP:

$$(PP) \quad \forall X \forall Y (\#^P(X) = \#^P(Y) \leftrightarrow [(\text{Inf}(X) \wedge \text{Inf}(Y)) \vee (\text{Fin}(X) \wedge \text{Fin}(Y) \wedge X \approx Y)].$$

PP is consistent with HP.[144] However, these principles cannot both be analytic of the *same* concept of cardinal number. PP entails that $\#^P(\mathbb{N}) = \#^P(\mathbb{R})$, since both $\mathbb{N}$ and $\mathbb{R}$ are infinite, whereas HP entails that $\#(\mathbb{N}) \neq \#(\mathbb{R})$, since they cannot be put into one-to-one correspondence. The question is whether the (hermeneutical) abstractionist has reasons to prefer HP over its good company of cardinality principles. Mancosu calls this the *Good Company* problem.[145]

Mancosu anticipates three responses to this problem. *(a.)* A *conservative* Neologicist will argue for HP being the only correct AP; however, the conservative needs to explain why only HP is correct, given that all other principles are both acceptable and sufficient to derive the axioms of PA^2. *(b.)* A *moderate* Neologicist might turn to a weaker and finite version of HP, namely Finite Hume (HPF), which states that if the cardinalities of X and Y are governed by HP if both concepts are finite, but is silent on the cardinality of infinite concepts. *(c.)* Finally, a *liberal* Neologicist claims that any AP sufficient to derive the axioms of PA^2 is acceptable for the purpose of reconstructing arithmetical knowledge.

Relatedly, MacBride (2000) argues that Neologicism must be understood as an (exclusively) reconstructive project. Precisely, MacBride claims that Heck's claim (1) is false, since Neologicism "has no hermeneutic concern" and it is

---

[144] Moreover, PP satisfies all the Neologicist criteria for acceptable abstraction Mancosu (2016, pp. 184–185): It is therefore a "good" companion of HP.

[145] To generate an infinity of good companions that raise the same concern, Mancosu formulates a principle that assigns (i) the same cardinal number a to each infinite and coinfinite concept (i.e. concepts $\mathscr{C}$ whose complement $\neg\mathscr{C}$ is infinite); (ii) a different cardinal number b to each infinite concept whose complement is a finite cardinality n; (iii) a third cardinal number c to each infinite concept whose complement is not of finite cardinality n; and (iv) cardinal numbers to finite concepts in the same way as HP for any natural number n.

only meant to establish a *modal* claim inasmuch as *"apriori* truth could flow from a logical reconstruction of arithmetical practice" (MacBride 2000, p. 157). According to MacBride, the Good Company problem is dissolved if all the argument shows is that HP is not implicit in ordinary arithmetical reasoning since this is not required for the success of the project.[146]

Summing up, we can distinguish between two claims that abstractionists can make: (i) HP is implicit in the ordinary concept of *cardinal number*, and, possibly, (ii) Frege's Theorem reflects the way in which basic arithmetical truths are actually apprehended. As regards (ii), at least Wright claims that "no one actually gets their arithmetical knowledge by second-order reasoning from Hume's Principle" (Wright 2020, p. 327). However, (i) must be retained if "the conclusions at the end of Frege's Theorem are indeed statements of the basic propositions of arithmetic, *viz.* arguing that the subject has not changed" (Shapiro 2009, p. 81; cf. also Blanchette 2012). Accepting (i) makes however the position vulnerable to the Good Company problem. As seen, abstractionists can respond by renouncing both (i) and (ii). In this case, however, the sentences of FA should be – as pointed out by Snyder et al. (2018) – *"about the natural numbers* as ordinarily understood, and not merely some isomorphic surrogate" (p. 58, italic in the original) in order for arithmetic to be a priori.

5.4 Epistemic Bad Company and Related Concerns

The question is now if the Neologicist account of arithmetical knowledge can be extended to other APs. As we saw in Section 2.8, abstractionism faces the *Bad Company* problem, which consists in distinguishing "good" principles, such as HP, from "bad" ones, such as BLV.[147] Over the years, a plethora of *criteria for acceptable abstraction* have been proposed to solve this problem.

However, the Bad Company problem becomes *ugly* once we consider the epistemology of abstraction (we borrow this term from Ebert and Shapiro (2009); ugly is worse than bad, as will become clear) – cf. also Payne (2013b). Specifically, let ACC be the set of acceptability criteria. The question is what is the epistemic status of the relevant criteria – that is, if a subject must know that an AP satisfies ACC to be warranted to stipulate AP. More bluntly: Does the subject have to be able to tell the AP apart from the bad ones in order to gain epistemically from it?[148]

---

[146] An objection to reconstructive abstractionism is presented, however, in Nutting (2018); according to Nutting, abstractionism fails to provide a reconstruction of how either actual or idealized subjects acquire arithmetical knowledge.

[147] Boolos (1998a), Dummett (1991, 1998); for an analogous formulation, see Weir (2003, p. 13).

[148] We owe this formulation to an anonymous reviewer.

Suppose that the answer is "yes." Some of the criteria that have been proposed so far are syntactic, and require a theory of syntax that is often as strong as PA^2 itself. These criteria may be, therefore, *imponderable* to the epistemic subject in the sense that the relevant criteria cannot be formulated prior to laying down some AP (Payne 2013b, p. 62). Other criteria are model-theoretic. At least some of these criteria may be *ineffable* to the subject in the sense that they require more set-theoretic resources than can be recovered by (acceptable) abstraction (Ebert and Shapiro 2009; Shapiro and Uzquiano 2016).[149]

Another option is that the epistemic subject is justified in believing that AP satisfies ACC if the subject either has enough evidence that AP is acceptable or, weakly, (s)he has an epistemic warrant absent defeaters to assume that AP complies with ACC. Wright's entitlement strategy is a version of this second claim. However, Ebert and Shapiro (2009) formulate an objection against both strategies. They consider a cardinality AP whose right-hand side states that X and Y must be equinumerous, and, if sentence Q is *false*, then it must also be the case that every X is a Y and vice versa, where Q is the ramsification of some complex mathematical truth, for example, Fermat's Last Theorem:[150]

$$(HP+Q) \quad \forall X \forall Y (\#X = \#Y \leftrightarrow [X \approx Y \wedge (\neg Q \rightarrow \forall x(Xx \leftrightarrow Yx))]).$$

Ebert and Shapiro argue that if the subject is justified in believing HP+Q because she has insufficient evidence against it, then "the Neologicist bypasses all the hard and ingenious work that Wiles did in establishing Fermat's last theorem" (p. 430). In particular, the subject may easily conclude that Q from HP+Q.[151] The subject can then notice that both HP and HP+Q are true in the model of PA^2, and therefore conclude that Q is true of the natural numbers. Claiming entitlement instead of a priori justification is not of much help: "Suppose that [the epistemic subject] stumbles across a complex AP A that is deductively equivalent to HP+Q but he has no idea of this equivalence and he sees no reason to believe that any of the known paradoxes might apply to the principles [...] this yields cheap knowledge that Q is true of the natural numbers" (p. 435).

Hale and Wright replied to this problem by claiming that HP+Q is not acceptable as long as one agrees that "the *avoidance of arrogance* is a crucial constraint on good abstractions and good implicit definitions generally"

---

[149] It is worth noting that the APs that are used to reconstruct set theory are often unacceptable in light of the known criteria (see Section 2.8); see Linnebo (2011), Shapiro and Weir (2000), and Studd (2016).

[150] The "ramsification" of a formula is obtained by substituting all the nonlogical terms in the formula with a variable of the same type bound by a universal quantifier.

[151] *Proof.* Assume that $\neg Q$; then, HP+$Q \rightarrow$ BLV.

(Hale and Wright 2009a, pp. 480–481, italic in the original). This reply can be glossed as follows.[152] Avoidance of arrogance bans stipulations that are not epistemically "responsible." However, anyone who is aware of Russell's paradox would also know that HP+Q is not true unless Q is true. The truth of Q can be proved in the standard way; at this point, however, the stipulation of Q would not improve the epistemic standing of the subject.

There are, however, two problems with this reply. First, as noticed by Ebert and Shapiro, "the more 'ignorant' a subject is, [...] the less work she has to do to maintain the entitlement" (p. 435). Second, for the reply to work, the *unacceptability* of some APs, e.g. BLV, must work as higher-order evidence against the acceptability of other principles, e.g. HP+Q. However, this view needs to be fully worked out, otherwise the unacceptability of a single principle could counts against all APs – which seems to be the heart of the epistemic Bad Company problem.

6 New Directions in Philosophical Abstractionism

Let's take stock. Abstractionism in the philosophy of mathematics can be spelled out as a mathematical and a philosophical project (Section 1).

Mathematical abstractionism relies on APs, that is, universally quantified biconditionals of this form:

$$\Sigma\alpha = \Sigma\beta \leftrightarrow \alpha \sim \beta,$$

with $\sim$ being an equivalence relation. Because of the threat of inconsistency (Section 2.3), APs must be handled carefully, and contemporary mathematical abstractionism has aimed to retain consistency without crippling their mathematical strength.

At the same time, APs show themselves to be rather flexible logico-mathematical tools. Different APs can be formulated as instances of schematic AP, which, modulo consistency, interpret (fragments of) arithmetic, real analysis, and set theory (Section 2).

Philosophical abstractionism, on the other hand, can be committed to an array of semantic, epistemological, and ontological views.

Semantically, expressions of the form "$\Sigma\alpha$" may be conceived of as either singular terms standing for objects of some kind, as referring to properties of higher-order entities, or as quantifiers of sorts (Section 3).

---

[152] Note that at least Hale and Wright (2000) argue that the avoidance of arrogance "derives entirely from a purely structural feature common to all Fregean abstractions" (p. 146).

The ontology of abstraction focuses on the existence and nature of the objects introduced on the left of APs (Section 4). As for their nature, we can distinguish between two general orientations, which we will refer to as *inflationism* and *deflationism*, standing at the opposite ends of the spectrum of philosophical abstractionism.

Inflationism is the view that APs should be interpreted as expressing a content that goes beyond the one of a material biconditional. Rayo's (2013) Trivialism, according to which APs are interpreted as "just-is"-statements, Linnebo's (2018) Minimalism, according to which APs are interpreted in terms of *sufficiency*, and the *ground-theoretic* interpretation of APs can all be considered as forms of inflationism (cf. Section 4.2.3).

Deflationism, more generally, is any view that asserts that abstract objects have no intrinsic nature: Anything can be the semantic value of a term introduced by an AP, provided that it belongs to a large enough domain. As we saw, Antonelli (2010a, 2010b), Boccuni and Woods (2020), and, more recently, Schindler (2021) have all proposed versions of deflationism.

The most influential version of contemporary abstractionism, that is, Hale and Wright's Neologicism, stands between inflationism and deflationism. On the one hand, Neologicists maintain that HP is a principle for the metaphysical individuation of cardinal numbers, which as such have no nature beyond the one that is given by HP itself (Hale and Wright 2008). On the other hand, they also claim that the left of HP embodies a "reconceptualization" of the content expressed on its right and, therefore, that there is "no gap for metaphysics to plug" (Hale and Wright 2009b, p. 193) between the equinumerosity of concepts and the identity and existence of their numbers.

From the epistemological point of view, abstractionists and especially Neologicists claim that APs can be known a priori, or at least blamelessly believed, as a result of their stipulation as implicit definitions (Section 5.3.1). They also claim that higher-order logic transmits this epistemic warrant to the consequences of APs (Section 5.3.2).

6.1 Abstractionist Structuralism

As emphasized by Boccuni and Woods (2020), the deflationist view is close to a form of *structuralism* in the philosophy of mathematics.[153]

Traditionally, abstractionism and structuralism are conceived of as competing views. For instance, while (most) abstractionists focus on the nature of the objects introduced by the left of APs as self-subsistent objects, in general,

---

[153] See e.g. Hellman and Shapiro (2018) for an introduction to mathematical structuralism.

structuralists focus on mathematical structures, so that the nature of mathematical objects is exhausted by the positions they occupy in these structures (Shapiro 1997, p. 72).

However, structures can be introduced by abstraction from systems of objects and their properties (Linnebo and Pettigrew 2014, Schiemer and Wigglesworth 2019).[154] Structuralists claim that two systems S and S' have the same structure if, and only if, they are isomorphic (Shapiro 1997, pp. 91–93). This identity criterion for structures corresponds to an AP (where "[S]" stands for the structure of system S):

(S) $[S] = [S'] \leftrightarrow S \cong S'$.[155]

Positions in a structure can be introduced in the following way:[156]

Definition 2 (Positions) *Given two systems S and S' and elements x of S and x' of S',*

$$[x]_S = [x']_{S'} \leftrightarrow \exists f (f : S \cong S' \wedge f(X) = x').$$

Finally, the domain of these positions can be defined as follows:

Definition 3 (Domain) *Given a system $S = \langle D, R_1, \ldots, R_n \rangle$,*

$$[D]_S = \{[x]_S | x \in D\}.[157]$$

Structural abstraction seems to water down the differences between abstractionism and structuralism. The convergence between these two orientations in the philosophy of mathematics can be detected by considering two main features of structuralism and abstractionism respectively. Structuralists are in general committed to the thesis that mathematical objects have no nonstructural properties (Schiemer and Wigglesworth 2019). Similarly, abstractionists and especially Neologicists claim that the nature of abstract objects is exhausted by what is entailed by APs (e.g. Hale and Wright 2008; cf. also Section 4.3). One way to bring these conceptions together by abstraction is to develop a theory of mathematical structures as objects introduced by APs of the form (S), which, as Linnebo and Pettigrew (2014, pp. 273–278) argue, entail the structuralist thesis.

---

[154] Cf. Reck (2018) for a historical overview and connections with Dedekind's abstractionism.

[155] Unrestricted structural APs are inconsistent with unrestricted SOL. Leach-Krouse (2015) provides a neat solution to carve out a class of consistent structural APs.

[156] Cf. Linnebo and Pettigrew (2014, pp. 474–475).

[157] Cf. Linnebo and Pettigrew (2014, pp. 474–475); see also Leach-Krouse (2015) and Reck (2018, pp. 125–127).

Despite traditionally being opposed to one another (Hellman and Shapiro, 2018), abstractionism and structuralism can be effectively combined. At the time of writing this volume, the entanglement with structuralism is one of the most promising directions in abstractionism in the philosophy of mathematics, which further witnesses to its lasting fruitfulness both from a mathematical and a philosophical perspective.

References

Antonelli, A. (2010a). The Nature and Purpose of Numbers. *Journal of Philosophy*, *107*(4), 191–212.

Antonelli, A. (2010b). Notions of Invariance for Abstraction Principles. *Philosophia Mathematica*, *18*(3), 276–292.

Antonelli, A., & May, R. (2005). Frege's *Other* Program. *Notre Dame Journal of Formal Logic*, *46*(1), 1–17.

Assadian, B. (2019). Abstractionism and Mathematical Singular Reference. *Philosophia Mathematica*, *27*(2), 177–198.

Assadian, B. (2023). Abstraction and Semantic Presuppositions. *Analysis*, *15*(3), 419–428.

Assadian, B., & Buijsman, S. (2018). Are the Natural Numbers Fundamentally Ordinals? *Philosophy and Phenomenological Research*, *99*(3), 564–580.

Bagaria, J. (2023). Set Theory. In E. N. Zalta, & U. Nodelman (Eds.), *The Stanford Encyclopedia of Philosophy* (Spring 2023 ed.). https://plato.stanford.edu/archives/spr2023/entries/set-theory/.

Batitsky, V. (2002). Some Measurement-Theoretic Concerns about Hale's "Reals by Abstraction." *Philosophia Mathematica*, *10*(3), 286–303.

Benacerraf, P. (1973). Mathematical Truth. *Journal of Philosophy*, *70*(19), 661–679.

Blanchette, P. (2012). *Frege's Conception of Logic*. Oxford University Press.

Blanchette, P. (2021). Frege on Caesar and Hume's Principle. In F. Boccuni, & A. Sereni (Eds.), *Origins and Varieties of Logicism: On the Logico-Philosophical Foundations of Logicism* (pp. 27–54). Routledge.

Boccuni, F. (2010). Plural *Grundgesetze*. *Studia Logica*, *2*(96), 315–330.

Boccuni, F. (2013). Plural Logicism. *Erkenntnis*, *78*(5), 1051–1067.

Boccuni, F., & Panza, M. (2022). Frege's Theory of Real Numbers: A Consistent Rendering. *Review of Symbolic Logic*, *15*(3), 624–667.

Boccuni, F., & Woods, J. (2020). Structuralist Neologicism. *Philosophia Mathematica*, *28*(3), 296–316.

Boghossian, P. A. (1996). Analyticity Reconsidered. *Noûs*, *30*(3), 360–391.

Boolos, G. (1984). To Be Is to Be a Value of a Variable (or to Be Some Values of Some Variables). *Journal of Philosophy*, *81*(8), 430–449. (Reprinted in Boolos 1998b, pp. 54–72)

Boolos, G. (1985). Nominalist Platonism. *Philosophical Review*, *94*(3), 327–344. (Reprinted in Boolos 1998b, pp. 73–87)

Boolos, G. (1987a). The Consistency of Frege's *Foundations of Arithmetic*. In J. Thomson (Ed.), *On Being and Saying: Essays in Honor of Richard Cartwright* (pp. 3–20). MIT Press. (Reprinted in Boolos 1998b, pp. 183–201)

Boolos, G. (1987b). Saving Frege from Contradiction. *Proceedings of the Aristotelian Society, 87*, 137–151. (Reprinted in Boolos 1998b, pp. 171–182)

Boolos, G. (1989). Iteration Again. *Philosophical Topics, 17*(2), 5–21. (Reprinted in Boolos 1998b, pp. 88–104)

Boolos, G. (1993). Whence the Contradiction? *Aristotelian Society Supplementary Volume, 67*, 211–233. (Reprinted in Boolos 1998b, pp. 220–236)

Boolos, G. (1998a). Is Hume's Principle Analytic? In R. Heck (Ed.), *Logic, Language, and Thought* (pp. 245–262). Oxford University Press. (Originally published under the name "Richard G. Heck, Jr." Reprinted in Boolos 1998b, pp. 301–314)

Boolos, G. (1998b). *Logic, Logic, and Logic* (Richard C. Jeffrey, Ed.). Harvard University Press.

Boolos, G., & Heck, R. K. (1998). *Die Grundlagen der Arithmetik*, §§82-3. In M. Schirn (Ed.), *The Philosophy of Mathematics Today* (pp. 407–428). Clarendon Press. (Originally published under the name "Richard G. Heck, Jr." Reprinted in Boolos 1998b, pp. 315–338)

Brandom, R. (1996). The Significance of Complex Numbers for Frege's Philosophy of Mathematics. *Proceedings of the Aristotelian Society, 96*(1), 293–315.

Burgess, J. P. (1998). On a Consistent Subsystem of Frege's *Grundgesetze*. *Notre Dame Journal of Formal Logic, 39*(2), 274–278.

Burgess, J. P. (2005). *Fixing Frege*. Princeton University Press.

Clark, M. J., & Liggins, D. (2012). Recent Work on Grounding. *Analysis Reviews, 72*(4), 812–823.

Cocchiarella, N. (1985). Frege's Double Correlation Thesis and Quine's Set Theories NF and ML. *Journal of Philosophical Logic, 14*(1), 1–39.

Cocchiarella, N. (1992). Cantor's Power-Set Theorem versus Frege's Double-Correlation Thesis. *History and Philosophy of Logic, 13*(2), 179–201.

Conti, L. (2020). Russell's Paradox and Free Zig Zag Solutions. *Foundations of Science, 28*(1), 1–19.

Cook, R. (2003). Iteration One More Time. *Notre Dame Journal of Formal Logic, 44*(2), 63–92.

Cook, R. (2017). Abstraction and Four Kinds of Invariance. *Philosophia Mathematica, 25*(1), 3–25.

Cook, R. (2019). Frege's Little Theorem and Frege's Way Out. In P. Ebert, & M. Rossberg (Eds.), *Essays on Frege's Basic Laws of Arithmetic* (pp. 384–410). Oxford University Press.

Cook, R. (2021a). Abstractionism in Mathematics. In *Internet Encyclopedia of Philosophy*. https://iep.utm.edu/abstractionism/.

Cook, R. (2021b). Logicism, Separation, and Complement. In F. Boccuni, & A. Sereni (Eds.), *Origins and Varieties of Logicism: On the Logico-Philosophical Foundations of Logicism* (pp. 289–308). Routledge.

Cook, R. (2023). Frege's Logic. In E. N. Zalta, & U. Nodelman (Eds.), *The Stanford Encyclopedia of Philosophy* (Spring 2023 ed.). https://plato.stanford.edu/archives/spr2023/entries/frege-logic/.

Cook, R., & Ebert, P. (2005). Abstraction and Identity. *Dialectica, 59*(2), 121–139.

Cook, R., & Linnebo, Ø. (2018). Cardinality and Acceptable Abstraction. *Notre Dame Journal of Formal Logic, 59*(1), 61–74.

Correia, F., & Schnieder, B. (2012). Grounding: An Opinionated Introduction. In F. Correia, & B. Schnieder (Eds.), *Metaphysical Grounding: Understanding the Structure of Reality* (pp. 1–30). Oxford University Press.

Demopoulos, W., & Bell, W. (1993). Frege's Theory of Concepts and Objects and the Interpretation of Second-Order Logic. *Philosophia Mathematica, 1*(2), 139–156.

deRosset, L., & Linnebo, Ø. (2023). Abstraction and Grounding. *Philosophy and Phenomenological Research, 109*(1), 357–390.

Doherty, F. (2021). The Ontology of Abstraction, from Neo-Fregean to Neo-Dedekindian Logicism. In F. Boccuni, & A. Sereni (Eds.), *Origins and Varieties of Logicism: On the Logico-Philosophical Foundations of Logicism* (pp. 349–371). Routledge.

Donaldson, T. (2017). The (Metaphysical) Foundations of Arithmetic? *Noûs, 51*(4), 775–801.

Dummett, M. (1973). *Frege: Philosophy of Language*. Duckworth.

Dummett, M. (1991). *Frege: Philosophy of Mathematics*. Harvard University Press.

Dummett, M. (1993). What Is Mathematics about? In A. George (Ed.), *The Seas of Language* (pp. 429–445). Oxford University Press.

Dummett, M. (1994). Chairman's Address: Basic Law V. *Proceedings of the Aristotelian Society, 94*, 243–251.

Dummett, M. (1998). Neo-Fregeans: In Bad Company? In M. Schirn (Ed.), *The Philosophy of Mathematics Today* (pp. 369–388). Clarendon Press.

Ebels-Duggan, S. (2015). The Nuisance Principle in Infinite Settings. *Thought: A Journal of Philosophy, 4*(4), 263–268.

Ebert, P., & Rossberg, M. (2016). Introduction to Abstractionism. In P. Ebert, & M. Rossberg (Eds.), *Abstractionism: Essays in Philosophy of Mathematics* (pp. 3–33). Oxford University Press.

Ebert, P., & Shapiro, S. (2009). The Good, the Bad and the Ugly. *Synthese, 170*(3), 415–441.

Eklund, M. (2006). Neo-Fregean Ontology. *Philosophical Perspectives, 20*(1), 95–121.

Felka, K. (2014). Number Words and Reference to Numbers. *Philosophical Studies, 168*(1), 261–282.

Ferreira, F. (2018). Zigzag and Fregean Arithmetic. In H. Tahiri (Ed.), *The Philosophers and Mathematics: Festschrift for Roshdi Rashed* (pp. 81–100). Springer.

Ferreira, F., & Wehmeier, K. F. (2002). On the Consistency of the Δ_1^1-CA Fragment of Frege's *Grundgesetze*. *Journal of Philosophical Logic, 31*(4), 301–311.

Field, H. (1980). *Science without Numbers: A Defence of Nominalism*. Princeton University Press.

Field, H. (1989). *Realism, Mathematics, and Modality*. Blackwell.

Field, H. (2005). Recent Debates about the A Priori. In T. S. Gendler, & J. Hawthorne (Eds.), *Oxford Studies in Epistemology Volume 1* (pp. 69–88). Oxford University Press.

Fine, K. (1995a). The Logic of Essence. *Journal of Philosophical Logic, 24*(3), 241–273.

Fine, K. (1995b). Senses of Essence. In W. Sinnott-Armstrong, D. Raffman, & N. Asher (Eds.), *Modality, Morality, and Belief: Essays in Honor of Ruth Barcan Marcus* (pp. 53–73). Cambridge University Press.

Fine, K. (2002). *The Limits of Abstraction*. Oxford University Press.

Fine, K. (2005). Our Knowledge of Mathematical Objects. In T. Z. Gendler, & J. Hawthorne (Eds.), *Oxford Studies in Epistemology* (pp. 89–109). Clarendon Press.

Fine, K. (2012). Guide to Ground. In F. Correia, & B. Schnieder (Eds.), *Metaphysical Grounding* (pp. 37–80). Cambridge University Press.

Florio, S., & Leach-Krouse, G. (2017). What Russell Should Have Said to Burali-Forti. *Review of Symbolic Logic, 10*(4), 682–718.

Florio, S., & Linnebo, Ø. (2021). *The Many and the One: A Philosophical Study of Plural Logic*. Oxford University Press.

Frege, G. (1879). *Begriffsschrift, eine der arithmetischen nachgebildete Formelsprache des reinen Denkens*. Halle: Louis Nebert. (Translated as *Concept Script, a formal language of pure thought modelled upon that of arithmetic*, by S. Bauer-Mengelberg in J. van Heijenoort (ed.), *From*

Frege to Gödel: A Source Book in Mathematical Logic, 1879–1931, Harvard University Press, 1967, pp. 1–82)

Frege, G. (1884). *Die Grundlagen der Arithmetik: eine logisch mathematische Untersuchung über den Begriff der Zahl*. Breslau: W. Koebner. (Translated as *The Foundations of Arithmetic: A Logico-Mathematical Enquiry into the Concept of Number*, by J. L. Austin, Oxford: Blackwell, 1980)

Frege, G. (1891). *Funktion und Begriff*. Jena: Hermann Pohle. (Translated as *Function and Concept* by P. Geach in Geach and Black (eds. and trans.) *Translations from the Philosophical Writings of Gottlob Frege*, Oxford: Blackwell, 1980, pp. 21–41)

Frege, G. (1893/1903). *Grundgesetze der Arithmetik: Band I/II*. Jena: Verlag Hermann Pohle. (Complete translation by P. Ebert and M. Rossberg (with C. Wright) as *Basic Laws of Arithmetic: Derived Using Concept-Script*, Oxford University Press, 2013)

Ganea, M. (2007). Burgess' PV Is Robinson's Q. *Journal of Symbolic Logic, 72*(2), 619–624.

Hale, B. (2000). Reals by Abstraction. *Philosophia Mathematica, 8*(2), 100–123. (Reprinted in Hale and Wright 2001a, pp. 399–420)

Hale, B. (2001a). A Response to Potter and Smiley: Abstraction by Recarving. *Proceedings of the Aristotelian Society, 101*(3), 339–358.

Hale, B. (2001b). Singular Terms (1). In *The Reason's Proper Study: Essays towards a Neo-Fregean Philosophy of Mathematics* (pp. 31–47). Clarendon Press.

Hale, B. (2001c). Singular Terms (2). In *The Reason's Proper Study: Essays towards a Neo-Fregean Philosophy of Mathematics* (pp. 48–71). Clarendon Press.

Hale, B. (2002). Real Numbers, Quantities, and Measurement. *Philosophia Mathematica, 10*(3), 304–323.

Hale, B. (2005). Real Numbers and Set Theory. Extending the Neo-Fregean Programme beyond Arithmetic. *Synthese, 147*(1), 21–41.

Hale, B. (2013). *Necessary Beings: An Essay on Ontology, Modality, and the Relations between Them*. Oxford University Press.

Hale, B. (2018). Essence and Definition by Abstraction. *Synthese, 198*(8), 2001–2017.

Hale, B. (2019). Second-Order Logic: Properties, Semantics, and Existential Commitments. *Synthese, 196*(7), 2643–2669.

Hale, B. (2020). Ordinals by Abstraction. In J. Leech (Ed.), *Essence and Existence: Selected Essays by Bob Hale* (pp. 240–255). Oxford University Press. (Reprinted in Boccuni, F. and Sereni, A. (Eds.), *Origins and Varieties of*

Logicism: On the Logico-Philosophical Foundations of Logicism. Ch. 11. Routledge. 2021.)

Hale, B., & Wright, C. (2000). Implicit Definition and the A Priori. In P. Boghossian, & C. Peacocke (Eds.), *New Essays on the A Priori* (pp. 286–319). Clarendon Press.

Hale, B., & Wright, C. (2001a). *The Reason's Proper Study: Essays towards a Neo-Fregean Philosophy of Mathematics*. Clarendon Press.

Hale, B., & Wright, C. (2001b). To Bury Caesar.... In *The Reason's Proper Study: Essays towards a Neo-Fregean Philosophy of Mathematics* (pp. 335–396). Clarendon Press.

Hale, B., & Wright, C. (2002). Benacerraf's Dilemma Revisited. *European Journal of Philosophy*, *10*(1), 101–129.

Hale, B., & Wright, C. (2008). Abstraction and Additional Nature. *Philosophia Mathematica*, *16*(2), 182–208.

Hale, B., & Wright, C. (2009a). Focus Restored: Comments on John MacFarlane. *Synthese*, *170*(3), 457–482.

Hale, B., & Wright, C. (2009b). The Metaontology of Abstraction. In R. W. David Chalmers David Manley (Ed.), *Metametaphysics: New Essays on the Foundations of Ontology* (pp. 178–212). Oxford University Press.

Hallett, M. (1984). *Cantorian Set Theory and Limitation of Size*. Clarendon Press.

Hawley, K. (2007). Neo-Fregeanism and Quantifier Variance. *Aristotelian Society Supplementary Volume*, *81*(1), 233–249.

Heck, R. K. (1996). The Consistency of Predicative Fragments of Frege's *Grundgesetze der Arithmetik*. *History and Philosophy of Logic*, *17*(1–2), 209–220. (Originally published under the name "Richard G. Heck, Jr.")

Heck, R. K. (1997a). Finitude and Hume's Principle. *Journal of Philosophical Logic*, *26*(6), 589–617. (Originally published under the name "Richard G. Heck, Jr.")

Heck, R. K. (1997b). The Julius Caesar Objection. In R. K. Heck (Ed.), *Language, Thought, and Logic: Essays in Honour of Michael Dummett* (pp. 273–308). Oxford University Press. (Originally published under the name "Richard G. Heck, Jr.")

Heck, R. K. (2000). Cardinality, Counting, and Equinumerosity. *Notre Dame Journal of Formal Logic*, *41*(3), 187–209. (Originally published under the name "Richard G. Heck, Jr.")

Heck, R. K. (2011a). *Frege's Theorem*. Oxford University Press.

Heck, R. K. (2011b). A Logic for Frege's Theorem. In *Frege's Theorem: An Introduction* (pp. 267–296). Oxford University Press. (Originally published under the name "Richard G. Heck, Jr.")

Hellman, G., & Shapiro, S. (2018). *Mathematical Structuralism*. Cambridge University Press.

Hodes, H. T. (1984). Logicism and the Ontological Commitments of Arithmetic. *Journal of Philosophy*, *81*(3), 123–149.

Hodes, H. T. (1990). Ontological Commitments, Thick and Thin. In G. Boolos (Ed.), *Method, Reason and Language: Essays in Honor of Hilary Putnam* (pp. 235–260). Cambridge University Press.

Hofweber, T. (2005). Number Determiners, Numbers, and Arithmetic. *Philosophical Review*, *114*(2), 179–225.

Hofweber, T. (2023). Refocusing Frege's Other Puzzle: A Response to Snyder, Samuels, and Shapiro. *Philosophia Mathematica*, *31*(2), 216–235.

Horsten, L., & Leitgeb, H. (2009). How Abstraction Works. In A. Hieke, & H. Leitgeb (Eds.), *Reduction – Abstraction – Analysis* (Vol. 11, pp. 217–226). Ontos Verlag.

Iemhoff, R. (2020). Intuitionism in the Philosophy of Mathematics. In E. N. Zalta (Ed.), *The Stanford Encyclopedia of Philosophy* (Fall 2020 ed.). https://plato.stanford.edu/archives/fall2020/entries/intuitionism/.

Jané, I., & Uzquiano, G. (2004). Well- and Non-Well-Founded Fregean Extensions. *Journal of Philosophical Logic*, *33*(5), 437–465.

Knowles, R. (2015). What "The Number of Planets Is Eight" Means. *Philosophical Studies*, *172*(10), 2757–2775.

Leach-Krouse, G. (2015). Structural-Abstraction Principles. *Philosophia Mathematica*, *25*(1), 45–72.

Linnebo, Ø. (2009a). Bad Company Tamed. *Synthese*, *170*(3), 371–391.

Linnebo, Ø. (2009b). Introduction. *Synthese*, *170*(3), 321–329.

Linnebo, Ø. (2010). Pluralities and Sets. *Journal of Philosophy*, *107*(3), 144–164.

Linnebo, Ø. (2011). Some Criteria for Acceptable Abstraction. *Notre Dame Journal of Formal Logic*, *52*(3), 331–338.

Linnebo, Ø. (2013). The Potential Hierarchy of Sets. *Review of Symbolic Logic*, *6*(2), 205–228.

Linnebo, Ø. (2016). Impredicativity in the Neo-Fregean Programme. In P. Ebert, & M. Rossberg (Eds.), *Abstractionism: Essays in Philosophy of Mathematics* (pp. 247–268). Oxford University Press.

Linnebo, Ø. (2018). *Thin Objects: An Abstractionist Account*. Oxford University Press.

Linnebo, Ø. (2022). Plural Quantification. In E. N. Zalta (Ed.), *The Stanford Encyclopedia of Philosophy* (Spring 2022 ed.). https://plato.stanford.edu/archives/spr2022/entries/plural-quant/.

Linnebo, Ø. (2023a). Platonism in the Philosophy of Mathematics. In E. N. Zalta, & U. Nodelman (Eds.), *The Stanford Encyclopedia of Philosophy* (Summer 2023 ed.). https://plato.stanford.edu/archives/sum2023/entries/platonism-mathematics/.

Linnebo, Ø. (2023b). Replies. *Theoria, 89*(3), 393–406.

Linnebo, Ø., & Pettigrew, R. (2014). Two Types of Abstraction for Structuralism. *Philosophical Quarterly, 64*(255), 267–283.

Linnebo, Ø., & Shapiro, S. (2017). Actual and Potential Infinity. *Noûs, 53*(1), 160–191.

Linsky, B., & Zalta, E. N. (2006). What Is Neologicism? *Bulletin of Symbolic Logic, 12*(1), 60–99.

Litland, J. E. (2022). Collective Abstraction. *Philosophical Review, 131*(4), 453–497.

MacBride, F. (2000). On Finite Hume. *Philosophia Mathematica, 8*(2), 150–159.

MacBride, F. (2003). Speaking with Shadows: A Study of Neo-logicism. *British Journal for the Philosophy of Science, 54*(1), 103–163.

MacBride, F. (2006). The Julius Caesar Objection: More Problematic than Ever. In F. MacBride (Ed.), *Identity and Modality* (pp. 174–202). Oxford University Press.

MacBride, F. (2016). Neofregean Metaontology. In P. Ebert, & M. Rossberg (Eds.), *Abstractionism: Essays in Philosophy of Mathematics* (pp. 94–112). Oxford: Oxford University Press.

MacFarlane, J. (2017). Logical Constants. In E. N. Zalta (Ed.), *The Stanford Encyclopedia of Philosophy* (Winter 2017 ed.). https://plato.stanford.edu/archives/win2017/entries/logical-constants/.

Mackereth, S. (in press). Neo-Logicism and Conservativeness. *Journal of Philosophy*.

Mackereth, S., & Avigad, J. (2022). Two-Sorted Frege Arithmetic Is Not Conservative. *Review of Symbolic Logic, 16*(4), 1199–1232.

Mancosu, P. (2016). *Abstraction and Infinity*. Oxford University Press.

Moltmann, F. (2013). Reference to Numbers in Natural Language. *Philosophical Studies, 162*(3), 499–536.

Moltmann, F. (2016). The Number of Planets, a Number-Referring Term? In P. Ebert, & M. Rossberg (Eds.), *Abstractionism: Essays in Philosophy of Mathematics* (pp. 113–129). Oxford University Press.

Moretti, L., & Wright, C. (2023). Epistemic Entitlement, Epistemic Risk and Leaching (1st ed.). *Philosophy and Phenomenological Research, 106*(3), 566–580.

Nolt, J. (2021). Free Logic. In E. N. Zalta (Ed.), *The Stanford Encyclopedia of Philosophy* (Fall 2021 ed.). https://plato.stanford.edu/archives/fall2021/entries/logic-free/.

Nutting, E. S. (2018). The Limits of Reconstructive Neologicist Epistemology. *Philosophical Quarterly, 68*(273), 717–738.

Panza, M., & Sereni, A. (2013). *Plato's Problem: An Introduction to Mathematical Platonism*. Palgrave MacMillan.

Panza, M., & Sereni, A. (2019). Frege's Constraint and the Nature of Frege's Foundational Program. *Review of Symbolic Logic, 12*(1), 97–143.

Parsons, T. (1987). On the Consistency of the First-Order Portion of Frege's Logical System. *Notre Dame Journal of Formal Logic, 28*(1), 161–168.

Paseau, A. C. (2015). Did Frege Commit a Cardinal Sin? *Analysis, 75*(3), 379–386.

Payne, J. (2013a). Abstraction Relations Need Not Be Reflexive. *Thought: A Journal of Philosophy, 2*(2), 137–147.

Payne, J. (2013b). *Expansionist Abstraction* (Unpublished doctoral dissertation). University of Sheffield.

Pedersen, N. J. (2016). Hume's Principle and Entitlement: On the Epistemology of the Neo-Fregean Program. In P. Ebert, & M. Rossberg (Eds.), *Abstractionism: Essays in Philosophy of Mathematics* (pp. 161–185). Oxford University Press.

Picardi, E. (2017). Michael Dummett's Interpretation of Frege's Context Principle: Some Reflections. In M. Frauchiger (Ed.), *Truth, Meaning, Justification, and Reality: Themes from Dummett* (pp. 29–62). De Gruyter. (Reprinted in Picardi 2022, Ch. 4)

Picardi, E. (2022). *Frege on Language, Logic and Psychology: Selected Essays* (A. Coliva, Ed.). Oxford University Press.

Plebani, M., San Mauro, L., & Venturi, G. (2023). Thin Objects Are Not Transparent. *Theoria, 89*(3), 314–325.

Potter, M., & Smiley, T. (2001). Abstraction by Recarving. *Proceedings of the Aristotelian Society, 101*(3), 327–338.

Potter, M., & Smiley, T. (2002). Recarving Content: Hale's Final Proposal. *Proceedings of the Aristotelian Society, 102*(3), 301–304.

Pregel, F. (2023). Neo-Logicism and Gödelian Incompleteness. *Mind, 131*(524), 1055–1082.

Quine, W. V. O. (1955). On Frege's Way Out. *Mind, 64*(254), 145–159.

Quine, W. V. O. (1970). *Philosophy of Logic*. Harvard University Press.

Rayo, A. (2002). Frege's Unofficial Arithmetic. *Journal of Symbolic Logic, 67*(4), 1623–1638.

Rayo, A. (2007). Ontological Commitment. *Philosophy Compass*, *2*(3), 428–444.

Rayo, A. (2013). *The Construction of Logical Space*. Oxford University Press.

Rayo, A. (2014). Reply to Critics. *Inquiry: An Interdisciplinary Journal of Philosophy*, *57*(4), 498–534.

Reck, E. (2018). On Reconstructing Dedekind Abstraction Logically. In E. Reck (Ed.), *Logic, Philosophy of Mathematics, and Their History: Essays in Honor of W.W. Tait* (pp. 113–138). College Publications.

Reck, E. (2020). Dedekind's Contributions to the Foundations of Mathematics. In E. N. Zalta (Ed.), *The Stanford Encyclopedia of Philosophy* (Winter 2020 ed.). https://plato.stanford.edu/archives/win2020/entries/dedekind-foundations/.

Reck, E. (2021). Dedekind's Logicism: A Reconsideration and Contextualization. In F. Boccuni, & A. Sereni (Eds.), *Origins and Varieties of Logicism: On the Logico-Philosophical Foundations of Logicism* (pp. 119–146). Routledge.

Reck, E., & Schiemer, G. (2023). Structuralism in the Philosophy of Mathematics. In E. N. Zalta, & U. Nodelman (Eds.), *The Stanford Encyclopedia of Philosophy* (Spring 2023 ed.). https://plato.stanford.edu/archives/spr2023/entries/structuralism-mathematics/.

Roeper, P. (2016). A Vindication of Logicism. *Philosophia Mathematica*, *24*(3), 360–378.

Roeper, P. (2020). Reflections on Frege's Theory of Real Numbers. *Philosophia Mathematica*, *28*(2), 236–257.

Rosen, G. (1993). The Refutation of Nominalism (?). *Philosophical Topics*, *21*(2), 149–186.

Rosen, G. (2010). Metaphysical Dependence: Grounding and Reduction. In B. Hale, & A. Hoffmann (Eds.), *Modality: Metaphysics, Logic, and Epistemology* (pp. 109–136). Oxford University Press.

Rosen, G. (2011). The Reality of Mathematical Objects. In J. Polkinghorne (Ed.), *Meaning in Mathematics* (pp. 113–131). Oxford University Press.

Rosen, G. (2016). Mathematics and Metaphysical Naturalism. In K. Clark (Ed.), *The Blackwell Companion to Naturalism* (pp. 277–288). Wiley Blackwell.

Rosen, G., & Yablo, S. (2020). Solving the Caesar Problem – with Metaphysics. In A. Miller (Ed.), *Logic, Language, and Mathematics: Themes from the Philosophy of Crispin Wright* (pp. 116–132). Oxford University Press.

Rumfitt, I. (2003). Singular Terms and Arithmetical Logicism. *Philosophical Books*, *44*(3), 193–219.

Rumfitt, I. (2018). Neo-Fregeanism and the Burali-Forti Paradox. In I. F. Rivera, & J. Leech (Eds.), *Being Necessary: Themes of Ontology and Modality from the Work of Bob Hale* (pp. 188–223). Oxford University Press.

Schiemer, G. (2021). Logicism in Logical Empiricism. In F. Boccuni, & A. Sereni (Eds.), *Origins and Varieties of Logicism: On the Logico-Philosophical Foundations of Logicism* (pp. 243–266). Routledge.

Schiemer, G., & Wigglesworth, J. (2019). The Structuralist Thesis Reconsidered. *British Journal for the Philosophy of Science, 70*(4), 1201–1226.

Schindler, T. (2021). Steps towards a Minimalist Account of Numbers. *Mind, 131*(523), 863–891.

Schirn, M. (2002). Second-Order Abstraction, Logicism and Julius Caesar. *Diálogos. Revista de Filosofía de la Universidad de Puerto Rico, 37*(79), 319–372.

Schirn, M. (2013). Frege's Approach to the Foundations of Analysis (1874–1903). *History and Philosophy of Logic, 34*(3), 266–292.

Schirn, M. (2023). Frege on the Introduction of Real and Complex Numbers by Abstraction and Cross-Sortal Identity Claims. *Synthese, 201*(6), 1–18.

Schroeder-Heister, P. (1987). A Model-Theoretic Reconstruction of Frege's Permutation Argument. *Notre Dame Journal of Formal Logic, 28*(1), 69–79.

Schwartzkopff, R. (2011). Numbers as Ontologically Dependent Objects: Hume's Principle Revisited. *Grazer Philosophische Studien, 82*(1), 353–373.

Schwartzkopff, R. (2015). Number Sentences and Specificational Sentences: Reply to Moltmann. *Philosophical Studies, 173*(8), 2173–2192.

Schwartzkopff, R. (2016). Singular Terms Revisited. *Synthese, 193*(3), 909–936.

Sereni, A. (2019). On the Philosophical Significance of Frege's Constraint. *Philosophia Mathematica, 27*(2), 244–275.

Shapiro, S. (1991). *Foundations without Foundationalism: A Case for Second-Order Logic* (Vol. 17). Clarendon Press.

Shapiro, S. (1997). *Philosophy of Mathematics: Structure and Ontology.* Oxford University Press.

Shapiro, S. (2000). Frege Meets Dedekind: A Neologicist Treatment of Real Analysis. *Notre Dame Journal of Formal Logic, 41*(4), 335–364.

Shapiro, S. (2003). Prolegomenon to Any Future Neo-Logicist Set Theory: Abstraction and Indefinite Extensibility. *British Journal for the Philosophy of Science, 54*(1), 59–91.

Shapiro, S. (2009). The Measure of Scottish Neo-Logicism. In S. Lindström, E. Palmgren, K. Segerberg, & V. Stoltenberg-Hansen (Eds.), *Logicism, Intuitionism, and Formalism: What Has Become of Them?* (pp. 69–90). Springer.

Shapiro, S., & Linnebo, Ø. (2015). Frege Meets Brouwer (or Heyting or Dummett). *The Review of Symbolic Logic, 8*(3), 540–552.

Shapiro, S., & Uzquiano, G. (2016). Ineffability within the Limits of Abstraction Alone. In P. Ebert, & M. Rossberg (Eds.), *Abstractionism: Essays in Philosophy of Mathematics* (pp. 283–307). Oxford University Press.

Shapiro, S., & Weir, A. (2000). "Neo-Logicist" Logic Is Not Epistemically Innocent. *Philosophia Mathematica, 8*(2), 160–189.

Shapiro, S., & Wright, C. (2006). All Things Indefinitely Extensible. In A. Rayo, & G. Uzquiano (Eds.), *Absolute Generality* (pp. 255–304). Oxford University Press.

Sider, T. (2007). Neo-Fregeanism and Quantifier Variance. *Aristotelian Society Supplementary Volume, 81*(1), 201–232.

Simons, P. M. (1987). Frege's Theory of Real Numbers. *History and Philosophy of Logic, 8*(1), 25–44.

Snyder, E. (2017). Numbers and Cardinalities: What's Really Wrong with the Easy Argument for Numbers? *Linguistics and Philosophy, 40*(4), 373–400.

Snyder, E., Samuels, R., & Shapiro, S. (2018). Neologicism, Frege's Constraint, and the Frege-Heck Condition. *Noûs, 54*(1), 54–77.

Snyder, E., Samuels, R., & Shapiro, S. (2022a). Hofweber's Nominalist Naturalism. In G. Oliveri, C. Ternullo, & S. Boscolo (Eds.), *Objects, Structures, and Logics* (pp. 31–62). Springer.

Snyder, E., Samuels, R., & Shapiro, S. (2022b). Resolving Frege's Other Puzzle. *Philosophia Mathematica, 30*(1), 59–87.

Snyder, E., & Shapiro, S. (2019). Frege on the Real Numbers. In P. Ebert, & M. Rossberg (Eds.), *Essays on Frege's Basic Laws of Arithmetic* (pp. 343–383). Oxford University Press.

Studd, J. P. (2016). Abstraction Reconceived. *British Journal for the Philosophy of Science, 67*(2), 579–615.

Studd, J. P. (2023). The Caesar Problem – a Piecemeal Solution. *Philosophia Mathematica, 31*(2), 236–267.

Tappenden, J. (1995). Geometry and Generality in Frege's Philosophy of Arithmetic. *Synthese, 102*(3), 319–361.

Tappenden, J. (2019). Infinitesimals, Magnitudes, and Definition in Frege. In P. Ebert, & M. Rossberg (Eds.), *Essays on Frege's Basic Laws of Arithmetic* (pp. 235–263). Oxford University Press.

Tennant, N. (1987). *Anti-Realism and Logic: Truth as Eternal.* Oxford University Press.

Tennant, N. (2022). *The Logic of Number.* Oxford University Press.

Thomasson, A. (2013). Fictionalism versus Deflationism. *Mind, 122*(488), 1023–1051.

Thomasson, A. (2014). *Ontology Made Easy.* Oxford University Press.

Urbaniak, R. (2010). Neologicist Nominalism. *Studia Logica, 96*(2), 149–173.

Uzquiano, G. (2009). Bad Company Generalized. *Synthese, 170*(3), 331–347.

Uzquiano, G. (2019). Impredicativity and Paradox. *Thought: A Journal of Philosophy, 8*(3), 209–221.

Väänänen, J. (2021). Second-Order and Higher-Order Logic. In E. N. Zalta (Ed.), *The Stanford Encyclopedia of Philosophy* (Fall 2021 ed.). https://plato.stanford.edu/archives/fall2021/entries/logic-higher-order/.

Visser, A. (2009). The Predicative Frege Hierarchy. *Annals of Pure and Applied Logic, 160*(2), 129–153.

Walsh, S. (2016). The Strength of Abstraction with Predicative Comprehension. *Bulletin of Symbolic Logic, 22*(1), 105–120.

Walsh, S., & Ebels-Duggan, S. (2015). Relative Categoricity and Abstraction Principles. *Review of Symbolic Logic, 8*(3), 572–606.

Wehmeier, K. F. (1999). Consistent Fragments of *Grundgesetze* and the Existence of Non-Logical Objects. *Synthese, 121*(3), 309–328.

Weir, A. (2003). Neo-Fregeanism: An Embarrassment of Riches? *Notre Dame Journal of Formal Logic, 44*(1), 13–48.

Wetzel, L. (1990). Dummett's Criteria for Singular Terms. *Mind, 99*(394), 239–254.

Wigglesworth, J. (2018). Non-Eliminative Structuralism, Fregean Abstraction, and Non-Rigid Structures. *Erkenntnis, 86*(1), 113–127.

Woods, J. (2014). Logical Indefinites. *Logique Et Analyse, 227*, 277–307.

Wright, C. (1983). *Frege's Conception of Numbers as Objects*. Aberdeen University Press.

Wright, C. (1990). Field & Fregean Platonism. In A. D. Irvine (Ed.), *Physicalism in Mathematics* (pp. 73–93). Springer.

Wright, C. (1998). On the Harmless Impredicativity of $N^=$ ("Hume's Principle"). In M. Schirn (Ed.), *The Philosophy of Mathematics Today* (pp. 339–368). Clarendon Press. (Reprinted in Hale and Wright 2001a, §10)

Wright, C. (1999). Is Hume's Principle Analytic? *Notre Dame Journal of Formal Logic, 40*(1), 6–30. (Reprinted in Hale and Wright 2001a, pp. 307–32)

Wright, C. (2000). Neo-Fregean Foundations for Real Analysis: Some Reflections on Frege's Constraint. *Notre Dame Journal of Formal Logic, 41*(4), 317–334.

Wright, C. (2004a). Intuition, Entitlement and the Epistemology of Logical Laws. *Dialectica, 58*(1), 155–175.

Wright, C. (2004b). Warrant for Nothing (and Foundations for Free)? *Aristotelian Society Supplementary Volume, 78*(1), 167–212.

Wright, C. (2007). On Quantifying into Predicate Position: Steps towards a New(Tralist) Perspective. In M. Leng, A. Paseau, & M. Potter (Eds.), *Mathematical Knowledge* (pp. 150–174). Oxford University Press.

Wright, C. (2014). On Epistemic Entitlement (II): Welfare State Epistemology. In D. Dodd, & E. Zardini (Eds.), *Scepticism and Perceptual Justification* (pp. 213–247). Oxford University Press.

Wright, C. (2016). Abstraction and Epistemic Entitlement: On the Epistemological Status of Hume's Principle. In P. Ebert, & M. Rossberg (Eds.), *Abstractionism: Essays in Philosophy of Mathematics* (pp. 134–161). Oxford University Press.

Wright, C. (2020). Frege and Logicism: Replies to Demopoulos, Rosen and Yablo, Edwards, Boolos, and Heck. In A. Miller (Ed.), *Logic, Language, and Mathematics: Themes from the Philosophy of Crispin Wright* (pp. 279–353). Oxford University Press.

Yablo, S. (2001). Go Figure: A Path through Fictionalism. *Midwest Studies in Philosophy*, *25*(1), 72–102.

Yablo, S. (2005). The Myth of the Seven. In M. E. Kalderon (Ed.), *Fictionalism in Metaphysics* (pp. 88–115). Clarendon Press.

Zalta, E. N. (1983). *Abstract Objects: An Introduction to Axiomatic Metaphysics*. D. Reidel.

Zalta, E. N. (2023). Frege's Theorem and Foundations for Arithmetic. In E. N. Zalta, & U. Nodelman (Eds.), *The Stanford Encyclopedia of Philosophy* (Spring 2023 ed.). https://plato.stanford.edu/archives/spr2023/entries/frege-theorem/.

Contributions

This Element is the outcome of common and equally shared work. The individual responsibility for the sections is assigned as follows: Francesca Boccuni wrote Sections 2 and 3, Luca Zanetti wrote Sections 4 and 5, and both authors contributed equally to Sections 1 and 6.

Acknowledgements

We thank Stewart Shapiro for his interest in this Element and for his unwavering support. We are also grateful to two anonymous reviewers for their valuable comments, which definitely improved both the style and the substance of this work. Øystein Linnebo provided generous feedback on Sections 2, 4 and 5. Pietro Lampronti read the final manuscript and pointed out several typos and infelicities.

Cambridge Elements ☰

The Philosophy of Mathematics

Penelope Rush
University of Tasmania

From the time Penny Rush completed her thesis in the philosophy of mathematics (2005), she has worked continuously on themes around the realism/anti-realism divide and the nature of mathematics. Her edited collection, *The Metaphysics of Logic* (Cambridge University Press, 2014), and forthcoming essay 'Metaphysical Optimism' (*Philosophy Supplement*), highlight a particular interest in the idea of reality itself and curiosity and respect as important philosophical methodologies.

Stewart Shapiro
The Ohio State University

Stewart Shapiro is the O'Donnell Professor of Philosophy at The Ohio State University, a Distinguished Visiting Professor at the University of Connecticut, and Professorial Fellow at the University of Oslo. His major works include *Foundations without Foundationalism* (1991), *Philosophy of Mathematics: Structure and Ontology* (1997), *Vagueness in Context* (2006), and *Varieties of Logic* (2014). He has taught courses in logic, philosophy of mathematics, metaphysics, epistemology, philosophy of religion, Jewish philosophy, social and political philosophy, and medical ethics.

About the Series

This Cambridge Elements series provides an extensive overview of the philosophy of mathematics in its many and varied forms. Distinguished authors will provide an up-to-date summary of the results of current research in their fields and give their own take on what they believe are the most significant debates influencing research, drawing original conclusions.

Cambridge Elements ☰

The Philosophy of Mathematics